T0301913

An Analysis of

T. S. Eliot's

The Sacred Wood
Essays on Poetry and Criticism

Rachel Teubner

Routledge
Taylor & Francis Group

LONDON AND NEW YORK

Published by Macat International Ltd
24:13 Coda Centre, 189 Munster Road, London SW6 6AW.

Distributed exclusively by Routledge
2 Park Square, Milton Park, Abingdon, Oxon OX14 4RN
605 Third Avenue, New York, NY 10017

Routledge is an imprint of the Taylor & Francis Group, an informa business

Copyright © 2017 by Macat International Ltd
Macat International has asserted its right under the Copyright, Designs and Patents Act
1988 to be identified as the copyright holder of this work.

The print publication is protected by copyright. Prior to any prohibited reproduction, storage in
a retrieval system, distribution or transmission in any form or by any means, electronic, mechanical, recording or otherwise, permission should be obtained from the publisher or where
applicable a license permitting restricted copying in the United Kingdom should be obtained
from the Copyright Licensing Agency Ltd, Barnard's Inn, 86 Fetter Lane, London EC4A 1EN, UK.

The ePublication is protected by copyright and must not be copied, reproduced, transferred,
distributed, leased, licensed or publicly performed or used in any way except as specifically
permitted in writing by the publishers, as allowed under the terms and conditions under which
it was purchased, or as strictly permitted by applicable copyright law. Any unauthorised distribution or use of this text may be a direct infringement of the authors and the publishers' rights
and those responsible may be liable in law accordingly.

www.macat.com
info@macat.com

Cataloguing in Publication Data
A catalogue record for this book is available from the British Library.
Library of Congress Cataloguing-in-Publication Data is available upon request.
Cover illustration: Etienne Gilfillan

ISBN 978-1-912302-86-4 (hardback)
ISBN 978-1-912127-41-2 (paperback)
ISBN 978-1-912281-74-9 (e-book)

Notice
The information in this book is designed to orientate readers of the work under analysis,
to elucidate and contextualise its key ideas and themes, and to aid in the development
of critical thinking skills. It is not meant to be used, nor should it be used, as a
substitute for original thinking or in place of original writing or research. References and
notes are provided for informational purposes and their presence does not constitute
endorsement of the information or opinions therein. This book is presented solely for
educational purposes. It is sold on the understanding that the publisher is not engaged
to provide any scholarly advice. The publisher has made every effort to ensure that
this book is accurate and up-to-date, but makes no warranties or representations with
regard to the completeness or reliability of the information it contains. The information
and the opinions provided herein are not guaranteed or warranted to produce particular
results and may not be suitable for students of every ability. The publisher shall not be
liable for any loss, damage or disruption arising from any errors or omissions, or from
the use of this book, including, but not limited to, special, incidental, consequential or
other damages caused, or alleged to have been caused, directly or indirectly, by the
information contained within.

CONTENTS

THE MACAT LIBRARY

The Macat Library is a series of unique academic explorations of seminal works in the humanities and social sciences – books and papers that have had a significant and widely recognised impact on their disciplines. It has been created to serve as much more than just a summary of what lies between the covers of a great book. It illuminates and explores the influences on, ideas of, and impact of that book. Our goal is to offer a learning resource that encourages critical thinking and fosters a better, deeper understanding of important ideas.

Each publication is divided into three Sections: Influences, Ideas, and Impact. Each Section has four Modules. These explore every important facet of the work, and the responses to it.

This Section-Module structure makes a Macat Library book easy to use, but it has another important feature. Because each Macat book is written to the same format, it is possible (and encouraged!) to cross-reference multiple Macat books along the same lines of inquiry or research. This allows the reader to open up interesting interdisciplinary pathways.

To further aid your reading, lists of glossary terms and people mentioned are included at the end of this book (these are indicated by an asterisk [*] throughout) – as well as a list of works cited.

Macat has worked with the University of Cambridge to identify the elements of critical thinking and understand the ways in which six different skills combine to enable effective thinking.
Three allow us to fully understand a problem; three more give us the tools to solve it. Together, these six skills make up the **PACIER** model of critical thinking. They are:

ANALYSIS – understanding how an argument is built
EVALUATION – exploring the strengths and weaknesses of an argument
INTERPRETATION – understanding issues of meaning

CREATIVE THINKING – coming up with new ideas and fresh connections
PROBLEM-SOLVING – producing strong solutions
REASONING – creating strong arguments

To find out more, visit **WWW.MACAT.COM.**

CRITICAL THINKING AND *THE SACRED WOOD*

Primary critical thinking skill: CREATIVE THINKING
Secondary critical thinking skill: REASONING

The Sacred Wood helped to reorientate arguments about the study of literature and its production by redefining the nature of tradition and the artist's relation to it.

At a time when 'traditional' had become a way of damning with faint praise by reference to the past, Eliot reinterpreted the term to mean something entirely different. Tradition is not, he argues, merely 'handing down', but, instead, is something to be obtained 'by great labour.' Grasping tradition entails making a huge effort to understand how the past fits together.

Seen thus, a literary and artistic tradition is not just a piece of the past. It 'has a simultaneous existence and composes a simultaneous order,' and is not just past, but present as well. For Eliot, 'art never improves;' it merely changes, and each part of the tradition is constantly being reinterpreted in light of what is added to the whole. The role of poets, in Eliot's view, is to subjugate their own personality, and become 'receptacles,' in which 'numberless feelings, phrases, images… can unite to form a new compound.'

This redefinition of poets' relations to their predecessors fundamentally redefined an important critical problem and can be seen a classic example of creative thinking.

ABOUT THE AUTHOR OF THE ORIGINAL WORK

Born in 1888 in the US state of Missouri, **Thomas Stearns (T. S.) Eliot** moved to England in 1914, where he lived for the rest of his life, working variously as a poet, a cultural and literary critic, an editor, and even a financier. Eliot's reputation as a literary critic soared after the publication of *The Sacred Wood* in 1920 and two years later his poem *The Waste Land* brought him huge recognition as a poet. He died in 1965 aged 76, hailed as one of the greatest poets of the twentieth century.

ABOUT THE AUTHOR OF THE ANALYSIS

Rachel Teubner teaches in the Department of Religious Studies at the University of Virginia. Her work focuses on the intertextual relationships between religious and literary works, and the representation of religious thought in poetry. She is completing work on a PhD focused on representations of religious thought and experience in literature, particularly in poetry. This includes interpreting authors such as Dante and Hopkins as readers of classical sources, as well as considering such 20th century poetic respondents to Dante as T.S. Eliot and James Merrill.

ABOUT MACAT

GREAT WORKS FOR CRITICAL THINKING

Macat is focused on making the ideas of the world's great thinkers accessible and comprehensible to everybody, everywhere, in ways that promote the development of enhanced critical thinking skills.

It works with leading academics from the world's top universities to produce new analyses that focus on the ideas and the impact of the most influential works ever written across a wide variety of academic disciplines. Each of the works that sit at the heart of its growing library is an enduring example of great thinking. But by setting them in context – and looking at the influences that shaped their authors, as well as the responses they provoked – Macat encourages readers to look at these classics and game-changers with fresh eyes. Readers learn to think, engage and challenge their ideas, rather than simply accepting them.

'Macat offers an amazing first-of-its-kind tool for interdisciplinary learning and research. Its focus on works that transformed their disciplines and its rigorous approach, drawing on the world's leading experts and educational institutions, opens up a world-class education to anyone.'

Andreas Schleicher
Director for Education and Skills, Organisation for Economic Co-operation and Development

'Macat is taking on some of the major challenges in university education … They have drawn together a strong team of active academics who are producing teaching materials that are novel in the breadth of their approach.'

Prof Lord Broers,
former Vice-Chancellor of the University of Cambridge

'The Macat vision is exceptionally exciting. It focuses upon new modes of learning which analyse and explain seminal texts which have profoundly influenced world thinking and so social and economic development. It promotes the kind of critical thinking which is essential for any society and economy. This is the learning of the future.'

Rt Hon Charles Clarke, former UK Secretary of State for Education

'The Macat analyses provide immediate access to the critical conversation surrounding the books that have shaped their respective discipline, which will make them an invaluable resource to all of those, students and teachers, working in the field.'

Professor William Tronzo, University of California at San Diego

WAYS IN TO THE TEXT

KEY POINTS

- T. S. Eliot is among the most important poets of the twentieth century.
- To understand T. S. Eliot's poetic aims, it's vital to explore the ideas he expressed in *The Sacred Wood*.
- *The Sacred Wood* is a landmark text for understanding the major literary movements of the twentieth century.

Who Was T. S. Eliot?

Thomas Stearns Eliot (1888–1965) was an American-born writer who moved to London in 1914 and remained there for the rest of his life, working as a poet, cultural and literary critic, editor, and financier. Nowadays Eliot is best known as a major twentieth-century poet, but his critical writing has also had a profound influence on other writers and thinkers. His literary theories became central concerns of modernism,* an important cultural movement of the early twentieth century. Modernists rejected the artistic values of the nineteenth century and looked for new ways of thinking about art and literature.

After moving to London, Eliot became friends with many of the writers, artists, and thinkers associated with modernism. Among them were the poet Ezra Pound* and the writer Virginia Woolf.* Eliot's own reputation as a significant figure started to grow in 1920, with the publication of *The Sacred Wood*. This collection of 13 essays of literary criticism was an instant success and turned him into an acclaimed literary critic.

Within two years, he had also been hailed as a major poet. Eliot's poem *The Waste Land* was published in 1922, the same year as James Joyce's* *Ulysses*. Experimental in style, it captured the sense of fragmentation in post-war Europe. Europe's population had been devastated, most survivors had lost loved ones, and the political structures and cultural values that had defined pre-war Europe had been shattered. They hadn't yet transformed into something new. Like *Ulysses, The Waste Land* came to be regarded as a defining text of literary modernism.

Eliot died in 1965 in London, but his poetry and literary criticism continue to influence literature today.

What Does *The Sacred Wood* Say?

The Sacred Wood came out in 1920 and is a collection of 13 of T. S. Eliot's early essays of literary criticism. Written between 1917 and 1920, they were first published as stand-alone pieces.

In the first essay in the collection, "The Perfect Critic," Eliot discusses how he thinks critics should judge a work of literature and why literary criticism is important. Eliot stresses that critics should have a profound understanding of the literature of the past. By the past, he means the literary tradition of the West, which had grown from the classical works of the Greco-Roman* world. He believes that the greatest writers were to be found in the Elizabethan Age* (1558-1603) and in the time of Dante* (1265-1321). For Eliot, the achievements of those writers far surpassed the work of the Romantics* of the nineteenth century.

Eliot says that when critics have a deep knowledge of this long literary tradition, they then have the necessary level of insight to critique new works. They are able to see how a new work compares with work that has come before, which in turn allows them to assess the value of the new work accurately.

Eliot argues that a critic should not base this assessment on his or her emotional response to a text, but rather on a thoughtful, critical analysis of it. He explores these themes in more depth in the next five essays, which he groups together under the title, "The Imperfect Critic."

After calling on critics to judge a work by assessing it against the work of the past, he moves on to discuss the role of the creative writer. He contends that writers, too, should measure their work in the same way and understand the literary tradition within which they write. Only by doing so can they achieve their full potential.

In *The Sacred Wood* Eliot writes primarily about poetry. He says that poems should display integrity and "impersonality." By integrity, he means that all the elements of a poem should work together—integrate—to create the meaning of that poem. In the same way, a piece of literature should integrate with the great body of literature that precedes it. It should be understood as part of that literary tradition. By impersonality, Eliot means that the poet should strip away his or her personality and emotions from the poem. The poem should have its own emotion. That was in direct contrast to the ideas of the Romantic tradition, which had valued individuality and self-expression.

To illustrate his arguments, Eliot looks at the work of individual authors. Each of the last seven essays in the book focuses on a different writer. Some of those writers are well-known: Dante,* Shakespeare,* Christopher Marlowe.* Others, like Algernon Charles Swinburne* and Philip Massinger* are more obscure. Eliot critiques their work, judging it by his standards of literary achievement. These critiques help to clarify what Eliot meant by great literature and on what grounds a literary work should be assessed.

Why Does *The Sacred Wood* Matter?

Eliot had experienced some success even before he published *The Sacred Wood*. The essays that make up the collection had already appeared in some of London's literary magazines, and he had also published several poems. They included the well-received "The Love Song of J. Alfred Prufrock," which first appeared in 1915.

It was *The Sacred Wood* that proved to be a pivotal moment in Eliot's career. An instant success, it turned him into one of the most highly regarded literary critics in London. Many of the ideas contained in the book went on to become hugely important to literary modernism. In turn, modernism affected other key literary movements of the twentieth century.

Eliot's arguments also set the stage for a major shift within literary criticism. When Eliot was writing *The Sacred Wood*, the people who produced literary criticism tended to be writers. But Eliot's ideas about the role of the critic—and the qualities of the critical mind—helped to change that. *The Sacred Wood* fueled the growing trend for academics taking on the critic's role.

Eliot is now seen as one of the greatest poets in the twentieth century, which explains why he is better known as a poet than as a critic. But to understand Eliot's poetic aims, it's vital to explore the ideas he expressed in *The Sacred Wood*. This is also extremely important in helping understand the poets who came after him. Eliot's influence was so great that his ideas influenced—directly or indirectly—most of the major English-language poets of the twentieth century.

Beyond poetry, Eliot's ideas have also been important in certain religious debates. He believed in tradition and the importance of integrating the present with the past, and these theories have been discussed in relation to change within the Anglican Church.

Political theorists also continue to debate Eliot's thinking. In *The Sacred Wood*, he argues that literature flourishes within particular intellectual cultures. These cultures, he says, are bound together by clear religious and philosophical values. In the early 1930s, Eliot expanded this theory into a discussion of what an ideal intellectual society might look like. These later ideas seemed sympathetic to Europe's emerging fascist* and nationalist* regimes, and as such they damaged Eliot's reputation. The literary world tends to regard Eliot's social and political comments as problematic.

Yet some influential political theorists have a different view. They point out that, in fact, Eliot rejected the ideologies of communism and fascism. Others have also noted that it's important to view Eliot's ideas within the context of his times. Eliot was writing before World War II* and before the full horrors of the Holocaust* had been revealed. Given that, his comments could be seen as naive. In the final analysis, *The Sacred Wood* remains a highly relevant text for people interested in political theory because it expresses ideas about the relationship between social frameworks and human achievement.

SECTION 1
INFLUENCES

MODULE 1
THE AUTHOR AND THE
HISTORICAL CONTEXT

KEY POINTS

- *The Sacred Wood* established T. S. Eliot's reputation as a literary critic and is an essential text for understanding his literary and cultural aims

- Although he rejected his family's Unitarianism* as an adult, Eliot was deeply shaped by his religious upbringing.

- The cultural context of early modernism* and the political context of World War I* exerted a major influence on the concerns of *The Sacred Wood*.

Why Read This Text?

The Sacred Wood is a collection of 13 essays of literary criticism that T. S. Eliot wrote between 1917 and 1920, while he was living in London. Although originally written as independent pieces, many of the same themes and ideas link the essays together. They include the value of "integrity"* in art, the importance of understanding what has gone before in the literary past, and the nature of the relationship between the artist and the critic.

Brought together in *The Sacred Wood,* the essays were an immediate success. The book established Eliot's reputation as one of the most influential and highly regarded critics in London. Modernists—writers of the time who were interested in breaking with recent literary conventions and redefining literary values—particularly responded to *The Sacred Wood*. Eliot's ideas about what made for a successful poem would go on to become defining concepts in literary modernism.

> ❝ Although Eliot at first sidestepped family morality
> in the name of art, he urged the claims of art with the
> same seriousness as his relatives advocated religious and
> social duty. ❞
>
> Eric Sigg, "Eliot as a Product of America" in *The Cambridge Companion to T. S. Eliot*

Nowadays, Eliot is better known as a poet than as a critic. But for anyone wanting to understand his literary and cultural aims, as well as the literary movements and important debates of the twentieth century, *The Sacred Wood* remains an essential text.

Author's Life

Despite spending most of his life in England, T. S. Eliot was actually American. He was born in 1888 in St. Louis, Missouri, and could trace his ancestry back to the early founders of New England. Eliot's grandfather, William Greenleaf Eliot, had left New England in the 1830s, moving west from Massachusetts to found a church in St. Louis. William Eliot was a Unitarian minister: a Christian who believed that God existed in one person, not three (Father, Son, and Holy Spirit). Rather than stressing the fact that Jesus Christ was a divine being, Unitarians emphasized the power of Christ's moral teachings. It was a religion that prized rationality over simple doctrines and the importance of reason ahead of worship.

The Eliot family remained in St. Louis throughout Eliot's childhood, but spent their summers in New England. This allowed them to retain important connections to the educational and religious culture of the eastern United States. Among the family's distinguished New England relatives were a number of notable American figures: the novelists Nathaniel Hawthorne* and Herman Melville* and the American presidents John Adams* and John Quincy Adams.*

Following both undergraduate and doctoral studies at Harvard University, a move to England in 1914, and marriage to Vivienne Haigh-Wood, Eliot accepted a post in the colonial and foreign department at Lloyds Bank in London. In 1917, he was invited to join the literary journal the *Athenaeum* as assistant editor. Most of the essays in *The Sacred Wood* were originally published in the *Athenaeum*. But even as Eliot started to build a literary reputation, he continued to work at Lloyds, developing his poetry and literary criticism outside of office hours. Biographical sources suggest that Eliot was under marital and financial strain, which is thought to have contributed to his decision to remain in steady employment throughout his early career.

By the time Eliot began to write the essays that would eventually be collected in *The Sacred Wood* (published in 1920), he had already distanced himself from his family's Unitarianism. But his background may have helped form some of his views, including his dislike of personal emotional expression and his belief in the importance of analysis. A theme that runs through *The Sacred Wood* is that *analysis*, rather than an emotional response to a work, is a crucial part of literary criticism. The collection also stated that poetry should present concrete, real images, which the reader can perceive, rather than simply be a vehicle through which to express the writer's emotions.[1]

Author's Background

Eliot started his own literary career in earnest around 1910, when skepticism toward nineteenth-century literary values was beginning to take hold. The Romantic* movement of that earlier period suggested that self-expression should be prized above all else. Romantic writers believed that an individual's personal response to something had huge value. Modernists criticized this attitude, arguing that the emphasis on personal emotion and individual response meant Romantic poetry was often lacking in ideas and intellectual content. The Romantics emphasized beauty in poetry: beauty of language, image, and poetic form. Their lofty style, dedicated to the appreciation of what was beautiful (aesthetics) seemed increasingly out of touch as the twentieth century got underway. The devastation of World War I only served to confirm that.

When war first broke out in 1914, the names, themes, and ideas that would be associated with modernism were just beginning to appear. But the romanticized portrayals of country life and dreamy visions that the Romantic Poets trumpeted seemed far removed from the devastations of wartime Europe. In the years that followed the war, Eliot—along with other modernist writers such as Ezra Pound* and Gertrude Stein*— would repeatedly try out new poetic styles. They explored new poetic forms, introduced disjointed rhythms, and used different techniques to create verse that was unified in its ideas, but fragmented in its form. That starkly differed from the Romantics, whose poetry had followed certain rules—for example, creating "perfect sonnets." But the fragmented style of the Modernists seemed to strike a chord as Europe struggled to comprehend the awful realities of the four years of the war from 1914 to 1918 and the breakdown of political and social structures.

In his 1928 preface to an updated version of *The Sacred Wood,* Eliot described the social and political environment between 1917 and 1920 as representing "a transition between the period immediately before the First World War and the period since."[2] The huge turmoil that resulted from the war defined the social and political climate. Eliot recognized that this war had had a huge impact on the people who survived it. Its horror had undermined their ability to cope with even everyday life. *The Sacred Wood* reflects a growing sense of unrest in society and of the failures of literature and culture to interpret and understand the realities of post-war Europe.

NOTES

1   Eric Sigg, "Eliot as a Product of America," in *The Cambridge Companion to T. S. Eliot*, ed. A. David Moody (Cambridge: Cambridge University Press, 1994), 15.

2   T. S. Eliot, *The Sacred Wood: Essays on Poetry and Criticism* (London: Faber & Faber, 1997), ix.

MODULE 2
ACADEMIC CONTEXT

KEY POINTS

- Literary criticism is concerned with how to assess the quality of a piece of writing.
- By the beginning of the twentieth century, modernists* had begun to challenge the values and achievements of nineteenth-century and Romantic* literature.
- Eliot believed that creative writers should have a deep understanding of the literary tradition in which they wrote. New work should be judged against the best work of the past.

The Work in its Context

The central purpose of the essays in T. S. Eliot's *The Sacred Wood* was to present ways of evaluating and appreciating works of literature. At the time that Eliot was writing, literary criticism was the work of writers, rather than academics. Samuel Taylor Coleridge* and Matthew Arnold* were England's greatest examples of writers-turned-critics, and members of the Bloomsbury Group* like Virginia Woolf* regularly undertook both creative and critical work. In the 1910s, these critics were questioning the aesthetics* of the nineteenth century, including the achievements of the Romantic Poets. They were introducing new principles and ideas about what made a poem beautiful or compelling that represented a break with the immediate past.

Overview of the Field

A question that is often asked is, "What makes a piece of art beautiful?" To complicate this issue, different people mean different things when

> **❝** ... The English poetry of the first quarter of [the nineteenth] century, with plenty of energy, plenty of creative force, did not know enough. This makes Byron so empty of matter, Shelley so incoherent, Wordsworth even, profound as he is, yet so wanting in completeness and variety. **❞**
>
> Matthew Arnold, "The Function of Criticism at the Present Time" in *Essays in Criticism*

they talk about beauty. Some focus simply on form: whether the work is visually or audibly appealing. Others use the discussion of beauty—aesthetics— to talk about what gives a piece of work value. In thinking about the value of a literary text, many writers and thinkers of the early twentieth century were influenced by the French philosopher Henri Bergson.* He drew on the scientific principles of observation and analysis to argue that writers should carefully look at what is around them and use the evidence of their senses to think about what they are experiencing. They should then convey those realities to their readers.

Bergson's ideas became a starting point for the Imagist* movement in poetry. The movement began in 1912 when Ezra Pound* declared the existence of a new school of poetry dedicated to Pound's "Doctrine of the Image." According to that manifesto, poetry should use concrete images that conjure up solid, tangible objects, or situations and that produce a definite sensation in the reader. The Imagist school of poetry dominated the London literary scene throughout the 1910s.

Those values of perception, concrete representation, and analytic rigor were all under discussion in the early twentieth century. Perception meant the reader's ability to grasp reality through a piece of writing. Concrete representation meant using real, tangible objects to help the reader seize on more abstract feelings or truths. And analytic rigor meant the writer's ability to analyze what he or she was seeing and sensing and then find a meaningful way of conveying that to a reader.

Eliot affirms those values in *The Sacred Wood*, so his work captures the spirit of his time. But he also broadened thought about literature. While some of his contemporaries sought to break from the past altogether, Eliot argues that, on the contrary, it was *vital* for writers to know what had come before them. A writer was, by definition, part of a literary tradition that went back centuries. By understanding his place in a long literary line, Eliot was able to bring a new perspective to his generation's criticism of the Romantics. He argues that writers should look at their own work in the context of the greatest writers of the past, particularly classical and Elizabethan works, rather than judging them against the Romantics of the nineteenth century alone.

At a time of when old ideologies were being questioned, Eliot developed a vision that affirmed, integrated, and broadened the literary sensibilities of Britain and America. This was one of the great achievements of *The Sacred Wood*.

Academic Influences

In the years leading up to the publication of *The Sacred Wood,* Eliot had studied in Paris and at the University of Oxford, completed a dissertation in philosophy at Harvard University, and immersed himself in the literary world of London. His studies in philosophy brought him into contact with Josiah Royce,* the Harvard philosopher who supervised his dissertation, and also made him familiar with F. H. Bradley,* the philosopher who became the subject of that dissertation.[1]

Royce and Bradley were known as pragmatic idealists. They believed it was important to find meaning in life and to develop a coherent framework for interpreting life. But the reason they believed those things were important was because having a sense of meaning and a framework within which to exist actually helped people to survive. Royce and Bradley did not argue for the pursuit of truth and meaning just for the sake of it. Pursuing truth and meaning had practical benefits. Eliot's view of tradition was similarly pragmatic. He valued the moral and cultural benefits that understanding the literary tradition could bring. Literature could help teach people how to live a rewarding life. It could also form one of the cultural links that help to bind societies together.

One can also see the ideas of English philosopher Bertrand Russell* in Eliot's work. The two men became close friends when Eliot was studying at Oxford in 1914. Russell's emphasis on critical rigor—careful, thorough thought and analysis—probably influenced Eliot's highly analytical approach to literature in *The Sacred Wood*.[2]

Eliot explicitly credited the French theorist Remy de Gourmont* as an influence. Gourmont said that sensation and perception should be central to literary criticism. Sensation refers to what we experience through our senses. Perception refers to the way we use those sensations to gather information. These are things that can be measured, so they can be analyzed. That means they can be objectively observed, so a critic can judge a work with a degree of objectivity, rather than relying on a more abstract inner reasoning.

Many of London's literary debates in the 1910s and 1920s were played out in journals devoted to the subject such as the *Athenaeum,* where Eliot was assistant editor for a time and where many of the essays in *The Sacred Wood* were first published. So the environments in which these debates happened were not academic. They took place in the world of the literary and cultural elite of London and, to a certain extent, among any English speakers who cared to read the articles.

NOTES

1   T. S. Eliot, Knowledge and Experience in the Philosophy of F. H. Bradley (London: Faber & Faber, 1964). Eliot's dissertation was accepted by Harvard College in 1916, but was published only in 1964, a year before his death.

2   Richard Shusterman, "Eliot as Philosopher" in *The Cambridge Companion to T. S. Eliot*, ed. A. David Moody (Cambridge: Cambridge University Press, 1994), 32–38.

MODULE 3
THE PROBLEM

KEY POINTS

- *The Sacred Wood* addressed some of the major questions of early modernism:* How should the greatness of a work of art be measured? What is the relationship of the artist to the work of art?

- When T. S. Eliot began writing, the literary world prized originality more than tradition.

- Eliot believed that the greatness of a work of art should be assessed in relation to the great art of the past. The artist should strive to express objective reality, not his or her own subjective experience.

Core Question

In the essays that make up *The Sacred Wood*, T. S. Eliot gives an extended answer to two questions at the heart of literary studies: what are the criteria according to which a work of literature should be analyzed and evaluated? And what is the proper relationship of the artist to the work of art?

Writers and critics have debated these matters ever since literature emerged as a distinct area of inquiry in the nineteenth century. Looking at the field of art and aesthetics* as a whole, those questions and discussions can be traced back to the poetics* of ancient Greek philosophy.

The Participants

In the London literary culture of the 1910s, matters of literature and art were generally the concern of writers and critics, rather than of

> **"** As an experimental writer who had at first found it difficult even to publish his verse, much less earn critical or popular favor, Eliot was aware that 'traditional' ways of interpreting poetry only hindered his generation of writers. He therefore looked for a way that artists could be 'judged by the standards of the past' but not 'amputated' by them. **"**
>
> Timothy Materer, "Eliot's critical programme" in *The Cambridge Companion to T. S. Eliot*

philosophers or academics. That was because literary criticism had emerged as a part of the literary profession. Widely circulated literary magazines were used as a forum for such debates, so *writers* usually wrote reflections on literature in that era. What they wrote was based on their own experiences as both writers and readers.

By the time Eliot began to write the essays that would become *The Sacred Wood,* he already had a small reputation in the literary world. He'd also become friendly with the poet Ezra Pound,* who was one of the leaders of a school of poetry called Imagism* in the 1910s. Imagists emphasized that poets should present visual images in their poetry. People who were drawn to Imagism believed that poetry should use regular language and concrete descriptions, images that could be visualized in the mind. This directness of presentation and economy of language had more in common with earlier classical poetry than the Romantic works of the late nineteenth century.

What made *The Sacred Wood* a groundbreaking book when it was published was the way Eliot blended the new ideas and concerns of modernism with a deep respect for the achievements of the past. He explores this idea in one essay in particular, "Tradition and the Individual Talent." In it, Eliot discusses his concept of "tradition": the idea that any poet is, by definition, part of a great poetic tradition, and his or her work needs to be judged and understood as part of that tradition. It has been suggested that Eliot derived his concept of tradition in part from Pound.[1]

In that same decade, Eliot also became friendly with members of the Bloomsbury Group,* which included Virginia and Leonard Woolf.* This London-based set of influential writers, artists, and intellectuals played an important role in the city's literary debates, and the group shared an interest in breaking with nineteenth-century aesthetics. They aspired to new literary and artistic ideals. The general interest in these issues set the stage for Eliot's argument in *The Sacred Wood*. Many people felt that artists should reject the works of the nineteenth century. But before Eliot, no one had been able to define how to relate to the wider literary past.

The Contemporary Debate

Eliot's philosophy teachers and colleagues were important in shaping his thinking about perception, sensation, and critical rigor as key aspects of literary criticism. But Eliot mainly addresses his arguments in *The Sacred Wood* to members of London's literary and cultural elite. In his introduction to *The Sacred Wood*, he cites the nineteenth-century English literary critic Matthew Arnold.* Arnold's view was that the work of the Romantic poets* didn't contain enough ideas or intellectual content. Eliot uses that judgment as the basis for emphasizing that *analysis* is crucial to criticism. Arnold's arguments also related to another of Eliot's key points: that any creative work is produced within a particular intellectual culture, and that culture strongly influences the work itself.

In *The Sacred Wood*, Eliot brings together in one place many of the concerns of early twentieth-century literature and philosophy. The work stands out because it represents a much broader and more mature vision of literary culture and tradition than his contemporaries and colleagues had previously put forward.

NOTES

1   Jean-Michel Rabaté, "Tradition and T. S. Eliot," in *The Cambridge Companion to T. S. Eliot*, ed. A. David Moody (Cambridge: Cambridge University Press, 1994), 214.

MODULE 4
THE AUTHOR'S CONTRIBUTION

KEY POINTS

- In *The Sacred Wood*, T. S. Eliot argues that the personality and feelings of the poet should not be evident in his or her poems. He calls this approach "impersonality."

- The Romantics* had seen poetry as about self-expression. Eliot's theory of impersonality was a complete break with Romantic values.

- Eliot was influenced by the ideas of the poet Ezra Pound* and the English philosopher F. H. Bradley.

Author's Aims

T. S. Eliot's literary analysis in *The Sacred Wood* is in many ways an argument against the Romantic poets. On the question of how literature should be analyzed, Eliot points out that the trend of criticism at the time was to search out (and value) what was *individual* in the work and thus what was *different* from the writer's predecessors. But Eliot argues that both writers and critics should evaluate works of literature in relation to the works of both the past and the present. It is only by looking at literature *as a whole,* he contends, that an assessment can be made of the quality of a new work.

Eliot's views on literature in *The Sacred Wood* stood apart from contemporary discussions of aesthetics* and literary judgments. His criteria for valuing a work of literature required knowledge not only of the work itself, but also of its relationship to the literary tradition.

Eliot also addresses the question of the relationship between the artist and the work of art. The Romantic ideal as set out by William Wordsworth* is that poetry is "emotion recollected in tranquility."*

66 We observe that we cannot define even the technique of verse; we cannot say at what point 'technique' begins or where it ends; and if we add to it a 'technique of feeling,' that glib phrase will carry us but little farther. We can only say that a poem, in some sense, has its own life; that its parts form something quite different from a body of neatly ordered biographical data; that the feeling, or emotion, or vision, resulting from the poem is something different from the feeling or emotion or vision in the mind of the poet. 99

T. S. Eliot, 1928 introduction to *The Sacred Wood*

After having an experience that provokes an emotion, Wordsworth believed poets should retreat and shape that emotional experience into a poem. Eliot disagrees. His view is that poetry should transform experience and emotion into art: something entirely different to the original experiences and emotions that prompted the poet to write. As part of this process, personal emotion should be removed from the poem. The final poem has, therefore, an emotion all of its own. This concept, which Eliot calls the "impersonality" of poetry, argues directly against the Romantics, whose poetry was preoccupied with expressing the emotions of the individual poets.

Approach

Eliot's concept of tradition added to a general school of thought among nineteenth-century writers that assumed literature drew from the material of the author's own emotion and experience. But Eliot's ideas laid out a standard for how literary modernists* ought to relate both to the past *and* to their own emotional lives and experiences. These ideas immediately became influential.

Ezra Pound had written about the interlinked nature of the great minds of all ages. The literary academic Jean-Michel Rabaté* suggested that Eliot may have used this idea to build his theory of tradition. But Eliot's concept is more wide reaching than Pound's. It includes *all* of the poetry that has ever been written, not only the great successes.

Eliot also makes a broader argument. He says that any given work of art draws on the culture within which it is created. As well as being part of a literary tradition, art is also part of an intellectual tradition shaped by morality, philosophy, and theology, among other things.

Eliot's linked concepts of tradition, integrity, and perception drew on emerging modernist understandings of what literary achievement actually was. He took contemporary objections to Romantic values and contemporary ideas about what poetry should do and transformed them into a sophisticated literary vision.

Contribution in Context

Eliot studied philosophy at Harvard University* between 1906 and 1909, and he focused his dissertation on the work of English philosopher F. H. Bradley.* Bradley believed that reality is made up of many interrelated parts. Each of those parts gets its meaning from its own individual place within reality, in much the same way that a group of individuals comes together to create a society. Each person forms a sense of self from his or her place within that society. Likewise a song is made up of many notes, but each note finds its meaning within the song as a whole.

Drawing on this idea, Eliot developed a concept of pragmatic idealism in his dissertation. His argument was that traditions help create understanding between the people who make up any given society. Traditions help to express ideas that each society has collectively agreed to be of value. One could view this as an early form of his argument in *The Sacred Wood* about the value of different works that literary tradition provides. Eliot believes that all the literary texts ever written created one organic whole. Evaluated in relation to one another, as part of this tradition, they could be ordered in terms of their relative greatness.

In the process of compiling *The Sacred Wood*, Eliot carefully revised his essays. Some of the revisions suggest a slight alteration in his views. For example, in the original version of the essay "The Local Flavour," Eliot argues that the American critic Paul More should not have brought issues of morality to the work of literary criticism. In *The Sacred Wood*, Eliot deletes that passage. As a result, the essay sits much better with his argument that there are clear relations between literature and culture, including religion and morality.[1]

Careful editing helped Eliot to integrate a broad range of influences and ideas in *The Sacred Wood*. He argues that literary and intellectual tradition should be seen as organically interrelated. The tradition comprised *all* literature and thought and requires a writer to actively study it and engage with it.

NOTES

1   David Huisman, "Title and Subject in *The Sacred Wood*," in *Essays in Criticism* (1989) XXXIX (3): 217–233.

SECTION 2
IDEAS

MODULE 5
MAIN IDEAS

KEY POINTS

- In *The Sacred Wood*, T. S. Eliot argues that all the poems ever written make up a "poetic tradition" with a "natural order" of greatness.

- New works find their place within this "natural order" of greatness. Their place naturally shows their literary value.

- *The Sacred Wood* presents its central ideas in a series of independent essays. They read as an extended argument for Eliot's concept of poetic tradition.

Key Themes

In *The Sacred Wood*, T. S. Eliot's central ideas of tradition, integrity, perception, and impersonality work together. They describe the poet's relationship both to the work of art that he creates and to poetic tradition. Eliot's views poetic tradition as "a living whole of all the poetry that has ever been written."[1] Certain works of poetry stand out as greater achievements than others, because the tradition possesses a natural order. When new works are written, they become part of the tradition and, in doing so, they change that tradition— even if only slightly.

Exploring the Ideas

The concept of *integrity* refers to the relationship between the part and the whole. A work of art integrates with all the other works of art that have come before it and is understood in relation to those other works. That concept of integrity is key to Eliot's understanding of tradition. But he also uses integrity as a way of evaluating individual works of

> ❝ What happens when a new work of art is created is something that happens simultaneously to all the works of art which preceded it. The existing monuments form an ideal order among themselves, which is modified by the introduction of the new (the really new) work of art among them. The existing order is complete before the new work arrives; for order to persist after the supervention of novelty, the *whole* existing order must be, if ever so slightly, altered; and so the relations, proportions, values of each work toward the whole are readjusted; and this is conformity between the old and the new. Whoever has approved this idea of order, of the form of European, of English literature, will not find it preposterous that the past should be altered by the present as much as the present is directed by the past. And the poet who is aware of this will be aware of great difficulties and responsibilities. ❞
>
> T. S. Eliot, "Tradition and the Individual Talent," *The Sacred Wood*

literature. Every element of a creative work, he says, helps to shape its final form—and its final form should be reflected in its parts. In *The Sacred Wood,* Eliot analyzes the work of different writers, using integrity as a measure of a work's literary value. He had learned the concepts of tradition and integrity as part of his philosophical training. What was original was the way that he applied them to literature.

It's also important to understand what Eliot saw as being the end purpose of poetry: by depicting things as they really are, it can help readers to contemplate reality and thereby live a more fulfilling life. The things depicted can be situations, objects, or chains of events. One example Eliot gives is the way in which Shakespeare uses the image of

Lady Macbeth walking in her sleep and trying to scrub imaginary specks of blood off her hands. That is a concrete image, but it conveys profound emotional and intellectual content, which the reader can perceive. This emphasis on *perception*—what the reader perceives—is key. Eliot cites as an example Dante's* *Divine Comedy.* This work transforms the emotional and intellectual material that makes up Christian theology, philosophy, and history into a complex and complete universe, which the reader can then perceive.

Perhaps Eliot's most complex concept in *The Sacred Wood* is that of *impersonality*—a concept based on the relationship between the artist and the work of art. Eliot argued that poetry should not be a vehicle for expressing a poet's emotions. Instead, the *poet* should be a vehicle for transforming emotions and experiences into works of art. A poem should be something truly original, from which all personal emotion has been removed. At that point, the poem is impersonal: it is its own being with its own emotion. The poet's personality has been sacrificed.

Language and Expression

Eliot originally wrote the essays in *The Sacred Wood* as separate works of literary criticism. As a result, one can read each essay as an independent piece of commentary and thought. For that reason, Eliot's themes do not appear in a logically structured way. They emerge from the essays organically when the book is read as an extended argument. The poetic and metaphorical qualities of Eliot's writing are likely to enrich the reader's appreciation of these ideas.

The theme of *tradition* is explained in the essay "Tradition and the Individual Talent." Here, Eliot argues that the poet must be deeply aware of the literary achievements of the past. These form a natural order that will be altered by the poet's new work. In Eliot's view, the critic's role is to preserve tradition. By doing so the critic can help contemporary poets see how their work relates to the great body of literary tradition.

Eliot also explores the theme of *impersonality* in "Tradition and the Individual Talent." He argues that the poet must surrender himself to the greatness of literary tradition. This involves a sacrifice of his or her own personality: poets sacrifice the fleeting preoccupations and emotions that affect only them in order to reflect the fundamental realities of life.

Many of the essays in *The Sacred Wood* discuss particular writers, from well-known authors like Shakespeare* and William Blake* to less well-known ones, like Algernon Charles Swinburne* and Philip Massinger.* Eliot uses the concept of *integrity* as a basis for analyzing and evaluating these writers. An excellent poem or play demonstrates integrity when its different elements all help the reader understand the poem as a whole.

Finally, the theme of *perception* is developed in the essay "The Perfect Critic." If a poet is conscious of poetic tradition, and a poem has both integrity and impersonality, then that poem can lead the reader to true contemplation of reality—of things as they really are. In Eliot's view, that is the ultimate purpose of poetry.

In *The Sacred Wood*, these themes come together in a vision of poetic tradition. Eliot demands that poets and critics be faithful to tradition and preserve it through study. He insists that contemporary literature should be measured according to the achievements of the past.

NOTES

1   T. S. Eliot, *The Sacred Wood: Essays on Poetry and Criticism* (London: Faber & Faber, 1997), 44.

MODULE 6
SECONDARY IDEAS

KEY POINTS

- The major secondary ideas in *The Sacred Wood* include T. S. Eliot's belief that the images and situations used by the poet should convey the meaning of the poem. He calls this the "objective correlative."*

- Eliot argues that a society's intellectual culture can support the creation of great art. Later in his life, he develops this idea into theories about "ideal" societies.

- Eliot's discussion about intellectual culture supports his broader vision of the importance of tradition.

Other Ideas

One of the major secondary ideas in *The Sacred Wood* is T. S. Eliot's concept of the "objective correlative." This refers to how successfully the techniques used by a poet create understanding for the reader. Do the images, gestures, and chain of events within the poem correlate with (i.e. match) the poem's objective (i.e. its intention)? This idea rested on Eliot's view that perception—or the true contemplation of reality—is the goal of poetry.

Other secondary ideas include Eliot's discussion of creative and critical minds and his treatment of the existing intellectual culture in which a work is created. This latter idea had implications that went beyond literature. But Eliot's intention was that the subject of *The Sacred Wood* should be " the problem of the integrity of poetry."[1] His ideas should therefore be seen primarily as principles for understanding literature, rather than any other discipline.

❝ The only way of expressing emotion in the form of art is by finding an 'objective correlative'; in other words, a set of objects, a situation, a chain of events which shall be the formula of that particular emotion; such that when external facts, which must terminate in sensory experience, are given, the emotion is immediately evoked. If you examine any of Shakespeare's more successful tragedies, you will find that the state of mind of Lady Macbeth walking in her sleep has been communicated to you by a skillful accumulation of imagined sensory impressions; the words of Macbeth on hearing of his wife's death strike us as if, given the sequence of events, these words were automatically released by the last event in the series. The artistic inevitability lies in this complete adequacy of the external to the emotion; and this is precisely what is deficient in *Hamlet*. ❞

T. S. Eliot, "Hamlet and His Problems," *The Sacred Wood*

Exploring the Ideas

In the essay "Hamlet and His Problems," Eliot argues that William Shakespeare's* *Hamlet*, one of his best-known plays, is actually a failure. Eliot makes this claim because *Hamlet* does not pass Eliot's objective correlative test. What's presented "externally" through the images and actions of the play does not match its emotional content.

Eliot's idea of the objective correlative is closely related to the Imagist* movement of the 1910s. The Imagists believed that poetry should present concrete objects in such a way that they produce an emotional reaction in the reader. What was original about Eliot was the way he applied this idea as the test of an entire play. This was so boldly original that it gave the concept added influence.[2]

Eliot's discussion of creative minds as compared to critical minds looks at the distinct roles that each of those minds should play in literary culture and achievement. Both sorts of mind, he argues, must have a historical sense of literature, which they should cultivate throughout their careers. Creative minds need to be conscious of tradition in order to surrender to it. Critical minds need to measure the achievements of the present against the whole of literary tradition. By doing so, they can help writers understand their place within that tradition.

Eliot argues that criticism should be an intelligent analysis of the sensations produced by a work of art. Just like the poet, the critic's work should be undiluted by emotions and based on perception. Such criticism is capable of illuminating a work of art and increasing its value for the reader. In doing so it can help lead to the ultimate goal of poetry: pure contemplation. It isn't clear exactly what Eliot means when he uses that phrase. It can be read as contemplation of God or deep consideration and reflection about the fundamental nature of reality. But Eliot believes such contemplation can help readers live more fulfilling, meaningful lives.

Eliot's treatment of intellectual culture—the thoughts and beliefs that frame a society—is, in many ways, an argument against what he saw as a lack of intellectual content in the literature of the nineteenth century. The Elizabethan age was Eliot's model for intellectual culture. Its literature showed "a very high development of the senses … when the intellect was immediately at the tips of the senses."[3] Elizabethan morals "provided a framework for emotions to which all classes could respond."[4]

Eliot also celebrates the age of Dante:* the end of the thirteenth century and the early part of the fourteenth century. He argues that, in Florence at that time, society worked within an intellectual, philosophical, and moral framework that everybody understood. It was part of daily life. That framework made it easier for Dante to state a vision of life in his poetry, which in turn helped to guide the reader into the state of contemplation.

Overlooked

One aspect of *The Sacred Wood* that has generally stayed in the shadow of these major themes is Eliot's focus on perception. He believes that perception—helping the reader to see things as they truly are—is essential to poetry. Perception is the key to contemplation of reality, which Eliot regards as the highest purpose of poetry. Eliot ends the first essay in the book, "The Perfect Critic," with a discussion of the end purpose of poetry, which he calls "a pure contemplation."[5]

He resumes that discussion in the final two essays of *The Sacred Wood*, "Blake" and "Dante". In those essays, Eliot describes Blake's and Dante's backgrounds and the cultural context in which they were working. He looks at the role that culture played in their poetry and how successful that poetry was in leading the reader into a state of contemplation. Eliot argues that William Blake's poetry suffered because he created his own mythologies.* Those mythologies weren't familiar to his readers, so they made his poetry harder to understand. If Blake had used a religious and mythological framework that was already known to his readers, Eliot says, it would have allowed him to concentrate on "the problems of the poet."[6]

Dante, in contrast, writing in medieval Italy, benefited from a theological framework that spread through all of life, according to Eliot. As a poet, he was able to unify the cultural beliefs of his time with the realities of life itself. That is what allowed Dante to offer a vision of life that leads the reader into a state of pure contemplation.

In *The Sacred Wood* Eliot seems to suggest that a society with a strong degree of cultural and moral unity is most conducive to producing great works of literature. Taken out of the context of literature, this discussion of intellectual culture can be tied to political theories that promote ethnic/cultural sameness. Later in his life, Eliot did voice some troubling political views; in the 1930s, he made a number of anti-Semitic comments that he later regretted. As a result, critics have tended to overlook his treatment of religion and theology within literary aesthetics.*

NOTES

1   T. S. Eliot, *The Sacred Wood: Essays on Poetry and Criticism* (London: Faber & Faber, 1997), x.

2   Louis Menand, *Discovering Modernism: T. S. Eliot and His Context*, 2nd ed. (New York: Oxford University Press, 2007), 134–139.

3   Eliot, *Sacred Wood*, 109.

4   Eliot, *Sacred Wood*, 114.

5   Eliot, *Sacred Wood,* 12.

6   Eliot, *Sacred Wood,* 134.

MODULE 7
ACHIEVEMENT

KEY POINTS

- T. S. Eliot's ideas about literary tradition, intellectual culture, and the relationship of the artist to the work of art were widely debated in the twentieth century.
- The major figures of literary London enthusiastically accepted *The Sacred Wood*.
- Eliot's political statements of the 1930s caused some people to reject his ideas.

Assessing the Argument

T. S. Eliot revised his essays before he included them in *The Sacred Wood*. The work doesn't have a single, overarching plan, but those revisions did allow a set of themes and concepts to develop over the course of the book.

In his introduction, Eliot suggests some—although not all—of those themes. He begins by quoting from the nineteenth-century English poet and critic Matthew Arnold.* Arnold praises the intellectual richness of ancient Greece and the Elizabethan age, and then goes on to lament the comparative lack of intellectual content in the work of the Romantic* poets of nineteenth-century England. Building on that, Eliot argues that it is the responsibility of the literary critic "to preserve tradition—where a good tradition exists." This involves examining the literature of the past *and* the present with the same critical mind in order to reveal the best of both. Eliot writes in this introduction that when critics do this, it is easier for creativity to flourish.

> ❝ The mystical experience is supposed to be valuable because it is a pleasant state of unique intensity. But the true mystic is not satisfied merely by feeling, he must pretend at least that he *sees*, and the absorption into the divine is only the necessary, if paradoxical, limit of this contemplation ... Dante, more than any other poet, has succeeded in dealing with his philosophy, not as a theory ... or as his own comment or reflection, but in terms of something *perceived*. ❞
>
> T. S. Eliot, "Dante," *The Sacred Wood*

Eliot develops those initial comments more thoroughly in some essays in *The Sacred Wood* than in others. His concept of tradition is clearest in the essay, "Tradition and the Individual Talent." He explores the roles of critic and poet in "The Perfect Critic" and in five essays gathered together as "The Imperfect Critic." In essays on Dante ("Dante") and Shakespeare* ("Hamlet and His Problems"), he examines the relationship between creativity and the broader intellectual culture.

Other essays in the book are not so easily linked to Eliot's key themes. Some deal with obscure authors, like Philip Massinger,* a lesser-known contemporary of Shakespeare's. Others introduce literary concepts that are difficult to define. These subjects make Eliot's arguments more challenging to follow than he may have thought.

Achievement in Context

Throughout *The Sacred Wood*, Eliot argues that literature flourishes when it exists within an intellectual culture that is understood by everyone. He emphasizes the importance of a culture's philosophical, religious and moral frameworks.

Eliot wrote *The Sacred Wood* in London after World War I.* In the aftermath of the horrors of that war, his comments can be understood as a reaction against the impressionistic, emotional, and individualistic tendencies of Romanticism in nineteenth-century poetry, and as a useful argument for building a rich intellectual culture. *The Sacred Wood* makes only a few proposals for what would be an *ideal* intellectual culture and contains no obvious ethnically or politically prejudiced content.

However, in the 1930s, Eliot publicly expressed views that seemed to lean toward the political ideology and anti-Semitism* of the Third Reich.* Many of Eliot's peers and critics found Eliot's cultural politics difficult. Then the atrocities of the Holocaust* during World War II* led some people, even as early as the 1940s, to view Eliot's cultural ideas as not simply indefensible, but actually immoral.

What certain critics have seen as instances of prejudice has affected Eliot's reputation. It can be difficult for modern readers to make allowances for his narrow cultural vision, even in its early form. Many of today's readers have found Eliot's cultural politics unforgiveable, given the multiculturalism of the late twentieth century—and the belief that a range of different beliefs and ethnicities can be accommodated within a single society. Others interested in Eliot's Anglo-Catholicism* have been unable to reconcile the same elements with a recognizable form of Christianity.

Some critics have dismissed Eliot's poetry altogether because of his perceived prejudices. Yet others have ignored his problematic cultural politics in favor of exploring his poetry dispassionately. Christopher Ricks* and Anthony Julius* are among the contemporary critics who have analyzed and criticized Eliot's anti-Semitism* while, at the same time, offering complex literary interpretations of his poetry.[1] As understood in its original context, it is perhaps appropriate to think of Eliot's early work as limited by the naivety of his time and place, and to read *The Sacred Wood* with that context in mind.

Limitations

Eliot wrote the essays that make up *The Sacred Wood* for publication in London literary journals, which had small but significant circulations. The majority of the writers and thinkers who formed his audience came from genteel families and studied at the Universities of Oxford or Cambridge. Critics and others began to view the fact that Eliot was surrounded by such a small and privileged group as something that limited his work and perhaps narrowed his ideas.

NOTES

1 Christopher Ricks, *T. S. Eliot and Prejudice* (Berkeley: University of California Press, 1988) and Anthony Julius, *T. S. Eliot, anti-Semitism, and literary form* (London: Thames & Hudson, 2003).

MODULE 8
PLACE IN THE AUTHOR'S WORK

KEY POINTS

- Throughout his literary career, T. S. Eliot was concerned with the relationship between art, the artist, and tradition.

- *The Sacred Wood* outlines themes that would occupy Eliot for several decades, both as a poet and a critic.

- *The Sacred Wood* has helped readers to interpret and appreciate Eliot's poetry.

Positioning

Although many of T. S. Eliot's critical essays had first appeared in the literary journal the *Athenaeum*, their publication as *The Sacred Wood* brought them a much broader readership, gaining attention on both sides of the Atlantic. The book launched debates about the relationship of the author to his or her work, the proper relationship between literature and culture, and the very purpose of literature itself. Eliot had already published a number of poems, including the well-received "The Love Song of J. Alfred Prufrock" (published in June 1915), but *The Sacred Wood* immediately established his reputation as a critic. For a time, Eliot was more highly regarded as a critic than as a poet, proving that the book was an extremely important landmark in Eliot's overall career.

Integration

In the years following the publication of *The Sacred Wood,* Eliot became renowned as a poet as well as a critic. The publication of *The Waste Land* in 1922 immediately established his reputation as a major poet and is generally hailed as a watershed moment in twentieth-century

> ❝ In my earlier criticism, both in my general affirmations about poetry and in writing about authors who influenced me, I was implicitly defending the sort of poetry that I and my friends wrote. This gave my essays a kind of urgency, the warmth of appeal of the advocate, which my later, more detached and I hope more judicial essays cannot claim. ❞
>
> T. S. Eliot, from his 1961 lecture, "To Criticize the Critic"

literature. In the 40 or so years of productive work that followed, Eliot turned his attention at various points to playwriting, social criticism, and social theory.

However, the ideas he developed in *The Sacred Wood* continued to shape his literary criticism. They also established a framework for interpreting the poetry and drama that he wrote throughout his career. In that sense *The Sacred Wood* was an argument, as Eliot later wrote, "for the sort of poetry that I and my friends wrote."[1] It was a manifesto as well as an instruction manual for appreciating the poetic style to which Eliot aspired.

Despite having been written at various points over three years, the essays in *The Sacred Wood* are more or less unified in their treatment of literary concepts and themes. In the main, they deal with literature itself, but the ideas expressed anticipate the shift that Eliot would gradually make towards dealing with social and cultural issues at large. In the essay "Tradition and the Individual Talent," Eliot argues that the poet must have a sense of tradition that involves knowledge of the past—knowledge that he or she must acquire over a lifetime of study and thought. The essay deals specifically with literature, but it anticipates the way in which Eliot's concept of "tradition" would broaden to include a wider cultural interest in the past.

Eliot's later critical works, such as *Notes Toward the Definition of Culture* (1938) and *The Idea of a Christian Society* (1939) developed these ideas further. But they did so in different and sometimes conflicting ways. The American literary critic Louis Menand* summarized Eliot's work through the 1920s and 1930s. He said it argued for classicism* in the form of "a pan-European culture, diversified according to language and regional tradition, but united as part of the civilization of Western Christendom." In the 1940s and 1950s, Eliot turned his attention to the new theme of "provincialism"— his term for the limitations and difficulties imposed on poets by their cultural and historical circumstances.[2]

Significance

Eliot's work had an immediate impact on the world of literature. The influence of *The Sacred Wood* and Eliot's early poems was so vast that it still reaches writers and readers today. Some read his work directly, while others encounter Eliot's influence through the great number of twentieth-century poets who responded to Eliot.

NOTES

1 T. S. Eliot, "To Criticize the Critic," in *To Criticize the Critic and Other Writings*, ed. Valerie Eliot (Farrar, Straus and Giroux, 1965), 16.

2 Louis Menand, *Discovering Modernism: T. S. Eliot and His Context*, 2nd ed. (New York: Oxford University Press, 2007), 175.

SECTION 3
IMPACT

MODULE 9
THE FIRST RESPONSES

KEY POINTS

- Many contemporary critics lauded *The Sacred Wood* for its scientific, analytical, and traditional approach to poetry.

- The severest and most enduring criticism of *The Sacred Wood* was that it encouraged cultural elitism.

- The belief held by some people that Eliot's cultural ideals were in sympathy with the fascist* and nationalist regimes of the 1930s made some of his ideas very unpopular.

Criticism

After *The Sacred Wood* was published in 1920, certain writers hotly contested T. S. Eliot's ideas about tradition and intellectual culture. The American poet William Carlos Williams* rejected Eliot as a cultural elitist. He contended that Eliot was highly educated, and *The Sacred Wood* seemed to suggest that all writers needed that level of education to produce anything of value. Williams also believed Eliot's proposed program to make poetry intellectually richer was damaging to the growth of poetry rooted in local culture.

By and large, however, university academics embraced Eliot's concepts. *The Sacred Wood* immediately became a central text in literature studies at both Oxford and Cambridge Universities.[1] Other writers, like the American poet Hart Crane,* were immediately impressed with Eliot's views on tradition and impersonality. Those views raised such writers' own aspirations to meet the literary requirements that Eliot set out in *The Sacred Wood*.

The common view in literary London was that Eliot represented the post-war re-emergence of literary values such as detachment,

> **❝** Leonard Woolf* was one of the first reviewers, and
> he reiterated the view that Eliot represented a post-
> war recovery of detachment. Writing in the *Athenaeum*,
> Woolf claimed that Eliot's work 'seems to cry aloud,
> "Back to Aristotle," and … brings us up with a shock
> against the satisfying, if painful, hardness of the intellect'
> … Woolf, like Pound, stressed the value of impersonality,
> quoting with approval Eliot's statement that 'it is in …
> depersonalization that art may be said to approach the
> condition of science.' **❞**
>
> Jewel Spears Brooker, in *T. S. Eliot: The Contemporary Reviews*

intelligence, and impersonality. Early reviewers of *The Sacred Wood,*
like the writer and critic Leonard Woolf, emphasized that view. They
approved of Eliot's scientific approach and the value of using methods
such as comparison and analysis. The American writer Conrad Aiken*
disagreed. He was one of the few critics at the time who took a stance
against Eliot's "scientific" approach, arguing that art can neither be
"impersonal" nor "scientific."[2] But the generally held view of *The
Sacred Wood*, particularly when considered alongside the success of
Eliot's early poetry, was that its author was fast becoming the leading
critic and poet of literary modernism.*

Eliot's concepts of impersonality and the objective correlative*
became cornerstones of the New Criticism,* a school of American
literary scholarship that became of major importance for much of the
twentieth century. In line with Eliot's ideas on impersonality, New
Criticism believed that a text should be studied on its own, without
looking for biographical or personal influences that may have
informed the writing. But in the 1970s, new types of literary
scholarship came to the fore that emphasized external influences on

texts, like the author's class or gender. As these ideas emerged, the Eliot-inspired literary theory of New Criticism fell out of favor.

The biggest blow to Eliot's reputation, however, resulted from his social and cultural ideas. Powerful fascist regimes emerged in Europe in the 1930s, followed by World War II.* Through the decades of political reflection that inevitably ensued, Eliot's cultural ideas became extremely unpopular. For instance, his vision of an ideal moral, intellectual, and religious culture appeared to be in line with the ideas of political fascism and nationalism*.[3] Eliot developed such social and cultural ideas, only faintly traceable in *The Sacred Wood*, in his later works. That commentary drew strong criticism for much of the twentieth century.

Responses

Most of literary London and the majority of university scholars accepted Eliot's emphasis on detachment and impersonality in literary criticism, together with a strong scientific approach. Some readers denounced the ideas in *The Sacred Wood,* but such criticisms didn't appear to have had any significant impact on Eliot or his career. He moved on quickly to other projects, including *The Waste Land*, published in 1922 and arguably his most famous and influential poem.

Later in his career, Eliot was recognized for reversing his earlier views. According to Louis Menand:* "The irony in the story of Eliot's influence on modern criticism is that even as his early judgments were being made the basis for new critical programs and revised literary canons, Eliot was already busy reversing them—so that he was, throughout his later career, frequently cited as an authority for arguments he had either repudiated or lost interest in."[4]

Conflict and Consensus

One can find only minor hints of cultural elitism in *The Sacred Wood*, but evidence of this viewpoint increases in Eliot's later social and cultural commentary. In the 1930s, Eliot developed a cultural blueprint for an ideal intellectual society. It appears dangerously sympathetic to emerging fascist and nationalistic regimes such as the Third Reich.* At a lecture at the University of Virginia in 1933, published as "After Strange Gods," Eliot also made comments that indicated a troubling anti-Semitism* in his intellectual vision.

After the horrors of the war and the Holocaust,* Eliot apologized for the content of this lecture. His focus changed in the 1940s and 1950s. He had converted to Anglo-Catholicism* and adopted more religious and communitarian* themes. Literary critics and others have sometimes interpreted poems such as "Ash Wednesday" and "Little Gidding" as having a conciliatory tone.[5]

Toward the end of his life, Eliot's cultural ideas faded into the background. His works returned to more enduring themes of art, religion, and social criticism. Eliot is still generally seen as one of the great literary influences on the Anglophone* world.

NOTES

1   Louis Menand, *Discovering Modernism: T. S. Eliot and His Context*, 2nd ed. (New York: Oxford University Press, 2007), 154.

2   Jewel Spears Brooker, *T. S. Eliot: The Contemporary Reviews* (Cambridge: Cambridge University Press, 2004), American Critical Archives series, xix–xx.

3   Jean-Michel Rabaté, "Tradition and T. S. Eliot," in *The Cambridge Companion to T. S. Eliot*, ed. A David Moody (Cambridge: Cambridge University Press, 1994), 210–211.

4   Menand, *Discovering Modernism*, 156.

5   Peter Dale Scott, "The Social Critic and his Discontents," in *The Cambridge Companion to T. S. Eliot*, 70–73.

MODULE 10
THE EVOLVING DEBATE

KEY POINTS

- T. S. Eliot's emphasis on detached, scientific, textual analysis influenced the way literary criticism developed.

- The New Criticism* was a school of literary criticism that was influenced by the ideas expressed in *The Sacred Wood*.

- Theologians* like Rowan Williams* have used the ideas of *The Sacred Wood* to discuss contemporary theological and ecclesiastical* questions.

Uses and Problems

Before T. S. Eliot's *The Sacred Wood* was published, literary criticism had mainly been the work of writers. Eliot's contemporaries, like Virginia Woolf* and other members of the Bloomsbury Group,* were involved in this work. But people in academic circles warmly received Eliot's belief that a "scientific" literary mind was important. Soon after the publication of *The Sacred Wood*, Eliot became established as the critic whom university academics liked best.

One of the long-term effects of Eliot's work has been the gradual establishment of literary criticism as an academic discipline. Louis Menand* points out that Eliot's success may be partly explained by his seizing of a cultural "moment ... when the sort of freelance, journal-based criticism practiced by members of the Bloomsbury Group was being displaced by a new, university-based type: the criticism of the academic with an interest in the condition of contemporary culture."[1]

> **❝** Eliot ... provided new ways of assuming voices, registering details, adapting speech rhythms, and putting elements together within poems. But his greatest genius, and greatest impact, lay in the ways that he allowed poets to cast technical experiment as significant cultural work struggling to make poetry a dynamic force for cultural change. **❞**
>
> Charles Altieri, "Eliot's impact on Anglo-American poetry," in *The Cambridge Companion to T. S. Eliot*

While such changes may already have been starting to happen, Eliot's arguments for a more scientific, analysis-based style of criticism may have played a role in this change. *The Sacred Wood* cemented his place as a defender of academic literary studies. Although journal-based literary criticism still goes on, since 1917 there has been a strong shift towards academic criticism. Today, most highly regarded critics are professors, rather than independent poets or artists. Although people have generally accepted this takeover by academics as being normal in our contemporary literary culture, some believe it has not been a good thing because it has cut off the world of literature from culture at large. Eliot is sometimes held responsible for this change.

Schools of Thought

The Sacred Wood had a strong influence on the modernist* movement in literature. Eliot's ideas attracted a great number of twentieth-century poets who aspired to follow his new principles for literary achievement. In addition, the literary aesthetics* that Eliot develops in *The Sacred Wood* became fundamental to New Criticism*—one of the most important literary criticism movements in the twentieth century.

In 1922, two years after the publication of *The Sacred Wood,* Eliot's poem *The Waste Land* appeared in London to immediate acclaim.

With its fragmented representation of experience and emotion, its use of multiple voices, and its near-constant references to art, religion, and philosophy, the poem both baffled and inspired its readers. Many felt *The Waste Land* brilliantly captured an historic "moment" of cultural confusion in Europe after World War I.* The poem built on the success of *The Sacred Wood* and helped establish Eliot as an authority in the world of literary criticism.

Few, if any, major twentieth-century poets writing in English could claim not to have been influenced by Eliot in some way. Several poets explicitly accepted Eliot's belief that poetry should be impersonal—that it should find emotion in the poem itself, rather than in the personal experience of the poet. The American poet Hart Crane* was a clear example of someone whom Eliot heavily influenced. According to the modernist scholar Charles Altieri,* "Crane … realized as early as 1919 that [modern poetry] would have to go 'through' Eliot … 'I would apply as much of his erudition and technique as I can absorb.'" Other important twentieth-century poets, such as W. H. Auden,* David Jones,* and Robert Lowell,* made similar statements about Eliot's immediate influence on their own work.[2] Clearly, Eliot not only had a significant impact on his contemporaries and his followers, but he has also continued to influence writers through the work of the many poets who took up his aesthetic principles.

The scholars most identified with *The Sacred Wood* are the literary critics who led the New Criticism movement. The Cambridge academic critics I. A. Richards* and F. R. Leavis* were both dedicated disciples of *The Sacred Wood* and crucial to the emergence of the New Criticism. From Eliot's literary principles, such as impersonality, integrity, and the objective correlative,* the New Criticism developed an analytical, text-based approach to literary analysis.

In the 1980s, New Historicism* replaced that movement. It emphasized the need to examine how historical and cultural circumstances influenced texts, rather than treating poems as independent works with their own integrity. The last 20 years have seen still another change, with New Formalism* emerging—a movement more closely aligned with Eliot's belief that form, detachment, and literary achievement are important. These waves of literary style and criticism suggest that, although *The Sacred Wood* is no longer a frequent reference point in literary debates, Eliot's concepts of impersonality and integrity endure as jumping-off points for the central questions of contemporary poetry.

In Current Scholarship

Nowadays, both theologians and literary scholars see value in *The Sacred Wood*. Among theologians, Rowan Williams, the former Archbishop of Canterbury, is perhaps the most important living scholar tackling the themes of *The Sacred Wood* and Eliot's work in general. For Williams, Eliot's theory of tradition and his view that individual personality should be sacrificed (in order to create something greater) are both related to Eliot's Anglican beliefs and his theological identity.

In the essay "Tradition and the Individual Talent," Eliot sets out a formula for the natural ordering of poetic tradition and the necessary surrender of the poet to that tradition. He wrote this essay in 1919, eight years before his conversion to Anglo-Catholicism.* But Williams views Eliot's concept of surrender as both literary and spiritual. He sees this notion as being as essential to Eliot's literary views as it would eventually be to his religious life.[3] In both cases, the views of the individual are less important than the judgments of tradition.

Eliot is only one among a great number of influences on Rowan Williams. Nonetheless, his theory of tradition certainly has an influence on Williams' own understanding of Church tradition. It has influenced Williams' views on the shifts and conflicts within the Anglican world. Like literature, the Church forms a whole made up of many individual parts. It has had to retain its integrity as the Church while absorbing many changes to the way Christianity is understood and practiced. Although Eliot may not have originally intended for his work to be interpreted in this way, his sympathy towards religious and moral culture can be seen in *The Sacred Wood*. Together with Eliot's eventual conversion to Anglicanism, this suggests that the author may not have been surprised or unhappy with where and how people are now discussing his work.

Within the world of literary scholarship, people such as Hugh Kenner* and Ronald Bush* have been major contributors to modern-day interpretations and appreciations of Eliot's life and work. Christopher Ricks* and Harold Bloom* have also done crucial work in rehabilitating Eliot's reputation as a canonical poet. To be part of the literary canon, an author's work must be considered to be among the most central works produced in their time. Ricks and Bloom have also made it clear that Eliot was a key force behind the flourishing of twentieth-century poetry in English.

The British attorney Anthony Julius,* best known as the legal representative of Diana, Princess of Wales, during her divorce proceedings with Prince Charles in1996, made his mark on the scholarly world by writing about Eliot. His work confronted the issue of Eliot's anti-Semitism,* while also arguing that anti-Semitism had provided material for his great achievements as a poet.[4]

Charles Altieri* is another important supporter of Eliot's poetics.* In the 1980s, a new school of literary criticism, New Historicism, emerged. This school displaced New Criticism and, at the same time, many scholars who had been heavily influenced by Eliot's writings. As a result, Eliot's literary theories fell out of favor. But Altieri defended Eliot. Although Altieri is less a disciple of Eliot than a scholar of American modernist* and postmodernist* poetics, he belongs to a school of literary scholars eager to reclaim Eliot in terms of the current trends in literary criticism, such as gender studies and postmodernist interpretation.

Scholars are now offering new readings of Eliot's work based on the issues that occupy them. Such studies are not likely to pay a lot of attention to *The Sacred Wood*, but they have still contributed to the gradual rehabilitation of Eliot's contribution to literary theory.

NOTES

1   Louis Menand, *Discovering Modernism: T. S. Eliot and His Context*, 2nd ed. (New York: Oxford University Press, 2007), 154–155.

2   Charles Altieri, "Eliot's impact on twentieth-century Anglo-American poetry," in *The Cambridge Companion to T. S. Eliot*, ed. A David Moody (Cambridge: Cambridge University Press, 1994), 190–191.

3   Rowan Williams, *Dostoevsky: Language, Faith, and Fiction* (Waco: Baylor University Press, 2008), 71.

4   Anthony Julius, *T. S. Eliot, anti-Semitism, and literary form* (London: Thames & Hudson, 2003).

MODULE 11
IMPACT AND INFLUENCE TODAY

KEY POINTS

- *The Sacred Wood* is a landmark text for modernist* studies, although individual essays are better known than the collection in full.

- Eliot's ideas of a "natural order" of artistic achievement remain relevant in debates about how the greatness of a work of art should be measured.

- Some scholars believe that works of art should be judged purely on their own merits. Others argue that the context in which they were written should influence how such works are viewed.

Position

Some critics have come to see T. S. Eliot's *The Sacred Wood* as holding a canonical* place in the study of literary modernism—as among the most central works produced in his time. The text is crucial to an understanding of the aesthetics* of that movement and its evolution through the twentieth century. At the same time, other critics and scholars often view *The Sacred Wood* as a work of literature in its own right, and those interested in the personal and spiritual insights that it contains frequently study it. A recent essay by American critic Anthony Domestico summarizes the text's central importance:

"It is fascinating to see Eliot work through his interests in poetic impersonality and the poet's relation to tradition, interests that would prove so important to modernist achievement in the 1920s. Just as valuable, however, is the sense that, in *The Sacred Wood*, we see a critic

> 66 Eliot was one of the most intellectually adroit of poets, a fine mind with a breadth of cultural and other knowledge that few writers since can equal or even attempt to emulate. He often felt humbled by the weight of all that had come before him; much of what he says in his essay, 'Tradition and the Individual Talent' is attractively modest in the limited program it proposes for poetry—not to explore ever finer and newer and more original emotion, but to find, through technique, a coldly rational way of honing language for its own sake, 'not the expression of personality but an escape from personality ... Only those who have personality and emotions can know what it means to want to escape from those things.' ... When we look at Eliot's writings on culture, we see a fine critical intelligence allied to a fear of possible consequences that is deeply terrifying in the way that ... elitist arrogance masquerades as humility and passionate concern to keep things as they are as a broadly accepting humanism. 99
>
> Roz Kaveney, *The Guardian*

growing into his voice, marshaling his myriad half-formed thoughts into arresting phrases and memorable aesthetic judgments."[1]

In considering the current treatment of *The Sacred Wood,* it is important to bear in mind, too, that the original text comprised 13 essays of literary criticism. They were not all groundbreaking. Yet several essays proved to be particularly influential, notably "Tradition and the Individual Talent" and "Hamlet and His Problems." Many readers may now read those more influential essays in the 1951 volume *Selected Essays* without even being aware of *The Sacred Wood*.

Interaction

Of the original set of essays, "Tradition and the Individual Talent" is the most influential, as well as the most widely read and discussed. Eliot's analysis of the individual writer's relationship to literary tradition has also been part of broader intellectual conversations. In addition, his Anglo-Catholicism* is of ongoing interest to the Church. Theologians* and religious biographers have frequently discussed the essay, using it as a way of illustrating the struggle that individuals can have to reconcile the Church's tradition and authority with their own religious beliefs.

The second chapter of Rupert Shortt's biography of Rowan Williams is called "Tradition and the Individual Talent."[2] By using this title, Shortt underpins his account of Williams' religious development with Eliot's concept of a living tradition that comprises all the monuments of the past. Shortt quietly builds a connection between the "great difficulties and responsibilities" that writers take on when they write a poem and the great burden that Church leaders take on when they take vows of fidelity to the Church. All of this is suggested without even mentioning Eliot's name.

Such references show the extent to which "Tradition and the Individual Talent," as well as *The Sacred Wood* itself, have been absorbed into contemporary intellectual culture. And the reasons for mentioning Eliot may be personal, professional, or political. As controversial as Eliot's later work has become, the central ideas of *The Sacred Wood* are still rich and admired enough that allusions to it can carry a weight similar to that of William Shakespeare* or the Bible. Rather than presenting a direct challenge to any one school of thought, *The Sacred Wood* serves as a reminder both of the importance of tradition and of the value in contributing to it—as Eliot himself set out to do.

The Continuing Debate

Over the past few decades, literary criticism and teaching have been concerned with the question of canonization. This is the process by which certain works achieve the status of "classics" or "great books." The word "canonization" itself suggests a fairly traditional model, and the works of white men have dominated the traditional canon. As such, people have criticized the canon as elitist—promoting, for instance, white authors instead of minority ones, and male writers instead of female writers. In doing so, its critics say that it ignores a huge amount of literary achievement.

As styles of literary criticism that emphasize the importance of external influences on creativity have emerged, scholars have increasingly tried to evaluate texts bearing in mind the possible influence of the social, cultural, and historical contexts in which they were written. They have often sought to elevate non-canonical voices, such as those of women and ethnic minorities, to a canonical status. But critics such as Harold Bloom* and Christopher Ricks* have taken up arms against the emergence of cultural, social, and post-colonial* criticism of the historic literary canon. They argue that it is important to isolate the literary elements of literature from those outside concerns.

In the context of this debate, Eliot's determination to consider "the problem of the integrity of poetry"[3] has been presented as evidence to support the traditional canon. So too has Eliot's desire to develop an analytical and purely literary method of criticism. His concept of tradition also contributes to the canonization debates, because it suggests literature itself will resolve the question of what is, and is not, great literature. In general, Eliot saw himself as an opponent of liberal progressivism.* He believed that an attitude of "progress for the sake of progress" was misguided and that it was important to recognize the best attributes of the past and to preserve them.

The arguments in *The Sacred Wood* were not intended to address the complexities of contemporary cultural and religious conflict— and thus are not equipped to do so. Eliot's own cultural politics and occasional anti-Semitic* remarks are now well known enough to invite a tide of criticism of his ideas and his writing. This means that even those critics who champion Eliot as a canonical writer tend to be cautious when talking about his literary theories, including the ideas discussed in *The Sacred Wood*. It would be unusual for *The Sacred Wood* to be championed as being able, on its own, to answer our present literary and cultural problems. But it continues to be one of many resources that are used as arguments for the preservation of a flourishing literary tradition.

NOTES

1   Anthony Domestico, "The Sacred Wood," *The Modernism Lab at Yale University*, accessed August 29, 2014, http://modernism.research.yale.edu/wiki/index.php/The_Sacred_Wood

2   Rupert Shortt, *Rowan's Rule: The Biography of the Archbishop of Canterbury* (Grand Rapids: Eerdmann's, 2011).

3   T. S. Eliot, *The Sacred Wood: Essays on Poetry and Criticism* (London: Faber & Faber, 1997), x.

MODULE 12
WHERE NEXT?

KEY POINTS

- *The Sacred Wood* contains hints of Eliot's later political thought. These ideas are still studied by political theorists.

- Eliot's concept of tradition is likely to remain fruitful for analyzing tradition within religious and theological studies.

- *The Sacred Wood* continues to be a useful text for understanding movements in twentieth-century literature in English, understanding Eliot as a literary and cultural figure, and understanding the work of other major poets of the twentieth century.

Potential

The Sacred Wood does not generally deal with the social and political arguments that would later occupy much of T. S. Eliot's energy. It has been mainly been used for literary exploration. But, at the same time, certain arguments in the work reflect Eliot's later interest in cultural politics and his conversion to Anglo-Catholicism.* Eliot's concept of tradition in *The Sacred Wood* demonstrates a great respect for the past—a belief that the past has greater value than the novelties of the present. From this attitude, it is possible to see how Eliot's later writing would grow. Here are the seeds of Eliot's doubts about the ideology of liberalism* and the hubris* of "progress" that characterizes his later writings about cultural politics.

The literary world now often regards Eliot's political views as problematic, believing that they tended towards communism* and fascism.* Scholars of political thought, however, have continued to debate the issue and have frequently painted a more moderate picture.

" If the only form of tradition, of handing down, consisted in following the ways of the immediate generation before us in a blind or timid adherence to its successes, 'tradition' should positively be discouraged. We have seen many such simple currents soon lost in the sand; and novelty is better than repetition. Tradition is a matter of much wider significance. It cannot be inherited, and if you want it you must obtain it by great labor. It involves, in the first place, the historical sense, which we may call nearly indispensable to anyone who would continue to be a poet beyond his 25th year; and the historical sense involves a perception, not only of the pastness of the past, but of its presence; the historical sense compels a man to write not merely with his whole generation in his bones, but with a feeling that the whole of the literature of Europe from Homer and within it the whole of the literature of his own country has a simultaneous existence and composes a simultaneous order. "

T. S. Eliot "Tradition and the Individual Talent," *The Sacred Wood*

For example, in *Eliot and His Age,* the American critic and historian Russell Kirk* argued that Eliot was a "consistent and intelligent opponent of both fascist and communist ideologies."[1] Kirk was also largely responsible for establishing Eliot's status as a contemporary intellectual hero by featuring him in one of his earlier works, *The Conservative Mind: From Burke to Eliot* (1953),[2] a founding text in American intellectual conservatism.*

Other recent explorations of Eliot's politics have highlighted his editorship of *The Criterion,** a London literary quarterly that he founded in 1922. Eliot's objective as the editor of this magazine was to provide disinterested political discussion,[3] and many of his readers believed he succeeded in his efforts.

Critics like Jason Harding* and Leon Surette* have focused on Eliot's dismissal of fascism and the political ideology of the Third Reich,* while also highlighting his eventual dedication to a positive set of religious beliefs: his conversion to Anglo-Catholicism.[4] These works are a useful resource to help understand Eliot both historically and intellectually and are also helpful guides to intellectual history and political thought in the twentieth century. In addition, their arguments contain many implications for current debates in culture and politics.

In 2013, the fourth volume of Eliot's collected letters was published, with the fifth volume following in late 2014.[5] These represent his correspondence from 1898 to 1931 and had been kept private after his death in 1965. The availability of these personal papers is likely to lead to new speculations about Eliot's early life and his intellectual development. Such explorations will presumably involve further work on understanding *The Sacred Wood* and the personal, spiritual, and cultural context in which it was written.

Future Directions

One area where scholars and others may further develop the core ideas of *The Sacred Wood* involves Eliot's concept of "tradition" as a living, organically ordered sum of all that has come before. In *The Sacred Wood,* Eliot's concept of tradition relates essentially to a poetic tradition. This is "a living whole of all the poetry that has ever been written,"[6] constantly altered by the addition of new poems and forming a natural order based on the greatness of each poem's achievement.

This concept, however, is easily extended beyond literature to other intellectual traditions, particularly philosophy, theology and religion. Recent work within the philosophy of religion has explored what a tradition actually is. It has also examined how change occurs when continuity is required. Western Christianity* is a good example. The Church in the West has changed a great deal over the centuries. Groups have broken away to form new religious bodies. Aspects of Church practice has been criticized and reformed. And yet the tradition of the Church has continued. In the context of these discussions, Eliot's treatment of tradition and intellectual culture may become a resource for further study in philosophy, theology, and history.

Since the appearance of *The Sacred Wood*, the academic world has become much more diverse. It has also become much more suspicious of traditional and hierarchical* definitions of culture. Many readers will reject Eliot's argument that an individual must be knowledgeable about the literature of the past if he or she wants to be a great writer or critic. The cultural changes that have occurred since *The Sacred Wood* was written, particularly the development of multiculturalism, will affect people's assessments of whether the book is still relevant. But it's still an engaging and challenging read. That alone may be enough to make *The Sacred Wood* a classic.

Summary

The Sacred Wood is likely to remain a living and influential text for several reasons. Eliot's status as one of the greatest poets in the twentieth century means that people will continue to explore his poetry and criticism. His influence on the development of twentieth-century literature means that core works like *The Sacred Wood* will still be used as a resource for understanding Eliot himself. Anyone interested in twentieth-century literature will want to investigate Eliot's intellectual development, his motivations and hopes, and his literary principles and religious convictions.

Moreover, *The Sacred Wood* is, in itself, a thoroughly readable and remarkable literary text. Despite the criticisms made of Eliot, it continues to engage its readers as a work of literature. With its direct style, lyrical precision, and intellectual breadth it remains an absorbing, even beautiful text, appealing to those who have any kind of interest in literature and writing. Regardless of the fact that the influence of Eliot's literary theory may be greater at some times than at others, *The Sacred Wood* will continue to reward anyone who is keen to explore his writing. It shows the poet as an ambitious young man of letters, determined to develop his creative and critical voice.

NOTES

1   Russell Kirk, *Eliot and His Age: T. S. Eliot's Moral Imagination in the Twentieth Century* (Wilmington: ISI, 2008), 132.

2   Russell Kirk, *The Conservative Mind: From Burke to Eliot,* 7th ed. (Wilmington: ISI, 2001).

3   Jason Harding, *The Criterion: Cultural Politics and Periodical Networks in Inter-War Britain* (Oxford: Oxford University Press, 2002).

4   Leon Surette, Dreams of a Totalitarian Utopia: Literary Modernism and Politics (Toronto: McGill-Queen's University Press, 2011).

5   T. S. Eliot, *The Letters of T. S. Eliot*, Vols. 1–4, eds. Valerie Eliot, Hugh Haughton, and John Haffenden (London: Faber & Faber, 2011–2013). T. S. Eliot, *The Letters of T. S. Eliot*, Vol 5: 1930–1931, eds. Valerie Eliot, T. S. Eliot, and John Haffenden (London: Faber & Faber, 2014)

6   T. S. Eliot, *The Sacred Wood: Essays on Poetry and Criticism* (London: Faber & Faber, 1997), 44.

GLOSSARY

GLOSSARY OF TERMS

Aesthetics: the philosophy of art and the beautiful, or a system of principles for the appreciation and valuation of the beautiful.

Anglo-Catholicism: a form of Anglican religious identity, belief, and practice that affirms the heritage and identity of the Roman Catholic Church. Although technically Protestant, Anglo-Catholicism affirms a "middle way" between the Roman and Anglican traditions.

Anglophone: in its literal sense, English-speaking. In literature, it refers to literature written in English; but the term in this context can also be used to refer to literature written outside of Great Britain and America to include writing from West and South Africa, India, and the Caribbean.

Anti-Semitism: a prejudicial bias against or hatred of Jews. Because of the Jews' unique status as an ethno-religious group, anti-Semitism is generally regarded as a form of racism. In Nazi Germany, anti-Semitism became a national political ideology and the basis for the program of extermination known as the Holocaust, but various groups and individuals have also expressed anti-Semitic views throughout the history of the Jewish people.

Bloomsbury group: an influential group of writers, artists, and intellectuals who lived and worked together near Bloomsbury, London, in the first half of the twentieth century. The group influenced modern attitudes toward literature, aesthetics, economics, feminism, and sexuality, and its most famous members include the novelist Virginia Woolf and the economist John Maynard Keynes.

Canonical: from the Greek, Kanon, refers to a rule of law. In Western culture, the term canon refers to the body of books and, more broadly, music and art that have been traditionally accepted by scholars as the most important and influential in shaping Western culture.

Capitalism: economic system based on private ownership of the means of production, private enterprise and the maximization of profit.

Christianity: major religion stemming from the life, teachings, and death of Jesus of Nazareth in the 1st century C.E. It has become the largest of the world's religions.

Classicism: a literary and philosophical orientation toward the study of "classics," generally meaning the works of classical Greek and Roman antiquity, as the standard of taste and judgment and the source from which all subsequent literature and philosophy derives.

Communism: a political ideology that relies on the state ownership of the means of production, the collectivization of labor, and the abolition of social class.

Communitarian: social and political philosophy emerging in the mid-nineteenth century that emphasizes the importance of community in the functioning of political life.

Conservatism: political doctrine that emphasizes the value of traditional institutions and practices.

The Criterion (1922–1939): London literary quarterly founded by T. S. Eliot in 1922 with the aim of setting a standard of intellectual and aesthetic judgment and creating a European intellectual community. As editor, Eliot published essays of literary, cultural, and social criticism.

Elizabethan age: epoch in English history of Queen Elizabeth I's reign (1558–1603). It was a time of great progress in the arts and stability in government, when a new sense of national identity developed, necessitated by the establishment of a national church. The era saw the first theaters in England, showing works of William Shakespeare and Christopher Marlowe.

Fascism: a radical political ideology that privileges the unity and power of a nation or race over the flourishing of the individual by means of a centralized, authoritarian state that aims to suppress all opposition. It came to prominence in Europe in the 1920s and 1930s in such nations as Germany and Italy.

Greco–Roman world: term used by modern scholars that refers to the geographical regions that were influenced by the language, culture, government, and religion of the ancient Greeks and Romans. Broadly, it refers to the Mediterranean world, which saw the spread of Greek culture by Alexander the Great, and later the spread of Christianity by the Roman Empire.

Hierarchy: in the social sciences, a ranking of positions of authority, often associated with a chain of command and control.

Holocaust (or Shoah): a genocide that took place during World War II under the government of Adolf Hitler within Germany and German-occupied territories in Europe. Jews living under German administration were a primary target of the Holocaust; homosexuals and people with mental and physical disabilities, along with many other ethnic minorities, were also persecuted.

Hubris: in Greek tragedy, excessive pride or self-confidence, usually an act of defiance against the gods, leading to nemesis or retribution.

Imagism: an early twentieth-century school of poetry that stressed colloquial language and concreteness of visual description and that played a defining role in literary modernism. Its defining principles were first set out by Ezra Pound in 1913; other poets who took up those principles included William Carlos Williams.

Integrity: term used by Eliot to mean that all the elements of a poem should work together—integrate—to create the meaning of that poem.

Liberalism: political doctrine that takes protecting and enhancing the freedom of the individual to be the central problem of politics.

Modernism: refers broadly to the cultural movement that developed at the end of the nineteenth century, and its aesthetics and principles. Writers in this period were concerned with breaking from the literary conventions, content, and styles of the nineteenth century and sought to redefine literary values.

Mythology: a collection of widely held beliefs that serves to explain the values of a given society.

Nationalism: ideology based on the premise that the individual's loyalty to the nation-state surpasses individual or group interests.

New Criticism: a major school of American literary scholarship that favored internal methods of reading texts, emphasizing the independence of the text from any biographical or personal influences and its formal and stylistic integrity.

New Formalism: championed by such poets as Dana Gioia and Marilyn Hacker, this was a school of American poetry in the late twentieth and early twenty-first centuries that favored a return to rhyme, meter, and other traditional conventions and techniques of poetry.

New Historicism: a school of literary criticism developed in the 1980s that practiced the interpretation of literature through its social, political, and historical context.

Objective correlative: a concept of balance between the intended emotion of a work of art and the events that evoke that emotion. In Eliot's words, "a set of objects, a situation, a chain of events which shall be the formula of that particular emotion; such that when external facts, which must terminate in sensory experience, are given, the emotion is immediately evoked."

Poetics: the area of literary criticism and theory that deals with poetry, its techniques, and aesthetics.

Postcolonial: critical movement in literature which analyzes the effects of colonization and imperial power on the production of culture and the formation of identity in colonized nations. Leading theorists include Edward Said, and leading authors include Chinua Achebe.

Postmodernism: a movement in literary studies, philosophy, and disciplines across the humanities and social sciences that developed following the modernist movements of the first half of the twentieth century. Postmodernism questions the assumptions and narratives of modernism and tends to criticize traditional hierarchies of knowledge, meaning, authority, and interpretation.

Pragmatism: an American school of philosophy originating around 1870. The core idea of pragmatism is that ideas can be clarified by testing their practical consequences.

Progressivism: political and social-reform movement that brought major changes to American politics and government during the first two decades of the twentieth century.

Romanticism: a poetic movement of the late eighteenth and early nineteenth centuries that prized nature and the interior world of feeling. Among the most celebrated English Romantic poets were William Wordsworth and Samuel Taylor Coleridge.

Theology: philosophically oriented discipline that studies the nature of God and religious beliefs.

Third Reich: also known as Nazi Germany, this refers to the administration of Adolf Hitler over Germany and German-occupied territory, which he governed as chancellor and then as dictator from 1933 until 1945. In 1939, Germany began to invade the nations of Europe, which led to the global conflict known as the World War II.

Unitarianism: a liberal religious movement that took hold in America in the late eighteenth century. Unitarianism rejects central Protestant theological tenets such as the doctrine of the Trinity, emphasizing the moral authority rather than the divinity of Jesus Christ. Although Unitarianism first developed in Europe, it is often regarded in the United States as an essentially American religion.

World War I (1914–1918): an international conflict centered in Europe and involving the major economic world powers of the day. The industrial advancements in military technology as well as the scale of the conflict resulted in vast military and civilian casualties, usually estimated at about nine million.

World War II (1939–1945): the most widespread military conflict in history, resulting in more than 50 million casualties. While the conflict began with Germany's invasion of Poland in 1939, it soon involved all of the major world powers, which gradually formed two military alliances and were eventually joined by the vast majority of the world's nations.

PEOPLE MENTIONED IN THE TEXT

John Adams (1735–1826) was the second president of the United States. He played a central role in the American Revolution, persuading Congress to declare independence from Great Britain and helping to write the Declaration of Independence.

John Quincy Adams (1767–1848) was the sixth president of the United States and son of the second American president, John Adams. His best-remembered achievements include the negotiation of the Treaty of Ghent, which brought an end to the War of 1812, and the authoring of the Monroe Doctrine (1823), which defined American foreign policy for over a century.

Conrad Aiken (1889–1973) was an American poet known for a flowing, Romantic style and psychological themes, as well as for his indifference toward literary fashion. He won the prestigious Pulitzer Prize in 1930.

Matthew Arnold (1822–1888) was a British poet and critic who addressed literary, social, and cultural issues in his criticism. Arnold is now commonly regarded as the most modern, and most sage, of the Victorian writers.

W. H. Auden (1907–1973) was an English poet, playwright, critic, and librettist. An émigré to the United States in the late 1930s, Auden's early work evidences a strong political and social context. Auden exerted a vast influence on twentieth-century poetry in English and won the Pulitzer Prize in 1948.

Henri Bergson (1859–1941) was a French philosopher whose combination of Darwinian theory and philosophy—and view of multiplicity, perception, and experience—were broadly influential on continental philosophy throughout the first half of the twentieth century.

William Blake (1757–1827) was an English poet, painter, and engraver. Unlike his contemporaries, he was born into a working family of moderate means and received almost no formal education. Blake's poetry stands out in this period as unconventional, dreamlike, and imaginative.

Harold Bloom (born 1930) is an American literary scholar, critic, and editor, and one of the most famous literary thinkers of his generation. He is best known for his work on Shakespeare and his defense of the traditional literary canon in *The Western Canon* (1994), as well as for such critical studies as *The Anxiety of Influence* (1973) and *The Anatomy of Influence* (2011).

Francis Herbert Bradley (1846–1924) was a British philosopher and the most prominent of the British Idealists, who responded to continental thinkers such as Georg Hegel (1770–1831) rather than to more popular British philosophers such as David Hume (1711–1776). Bradley's view of reality was interrelated and holistic, holding that things take meaning from their place within the single whole of reality.

Ronald Bush (born 1946) is a scholar of modernist literature, best known for his studies of James Joyce, Ezra Pound, and T. S. Eliot. He is currently Drue Heinz Professor of American Literature at Oxford University and Emeritus Research Fellow at St. John's College, Oxford.

Samuel Taylor Coleridge (1772–1834) was a pre-eminent poet-critic of modern English literature. His *Lyrical Ballads* (1798), a collaboration with William Wordsworth, became the defining text of the Romantic style, and his criticism is known for a wide-ranging intelligence and cultural influence.

Hart Crane (1899–1932) was an American poet known for a strand of American Romanticism that drew from the optimism of the American transcendentalists, such as Walt Whitman (1819–1892). Crane is regarded as a pivotal poet who captured the spirituality of American experience.

Dante Alighieri (1265–1321) was a medieval Italian poet, commonly known as Dante. He is best known for his *Commedia* or *Divine Comedy*, a long poem giving a first-person account of a pilgrim's journey through hell, purgatory, and paradise.

Remy de Gourmont (1858–1915) was a French poet, novelist, and literary critic of the Symbolist school, which rejected naturalism and realism in favor of dreams and visions. Best known for his critical work *Le Problème du Style* (*The Problem of Style*), which became a source for literary movements in England and France.

Anthony Domestico is an American writer and Assistant Professor of Literature at Purchase College, State University of New York.

Nathaniel Hawthorne (1804–1864) was an American author best known for his novels *The Scarlet Letter* (1850) and *The House of the Seven Gables* (1851). His writing was deeply influenced by the Puritan religious values of early nineteenth-century New England.

David Jones (1895–1974) was a Welsh poet, painter, and engraver, increasingly regarded as an innovative poet who refined the techniques of literary modernism.

Hugh Kenner (1923–2003) was a Canadian professor of literature and literary scholar. He became acquainted with Ezra Pound as a young man and went on to become one of the major critical interpreters of modernist literature. He is best known for his studies of Ezra Pound, James Joyce, and T. S. Eliot.

Russell Kirk (1918–1994) was an American political, social, and literary critic, as well as a historian and theorist known for his contributions to the founding of twentieth–century intellectual conservatism.

F. R. Leavis (1895–1978) was a British literary critic, teacher, and publisher who, with I. A. Richards, advocated for rigorous intellectual standards and often attacked what he saw as the informal dilettantism of the Bloomsbury Group.

Robert Lowell (1917–1977) was one of the most famous American poets of the twentieth century, known for a lyrical style and for helping to found the Confessional movement in American poetry. Lowell won the Pulitzer Prize in 1947.

Philip Massinger (1583–1640) was an English dramatist, who worked shortly after Shakespeare and thus is often viewed in light of Shakespeare's influence and legacy. His work is noted for its political insight and the memorable characters found in such plays as *A New Way to Pay Old Debts* (1625), *The City Madam* (1621–3), and *The Roman Actor* (1626).

Herman Melville (1819–1891) was an American writer, best known for his novel *Moby-Dick* (1851) and his unfinished novella *Billy Budd* (1924). Although little appreciated during his lifetime, Melville is now regarded as one of the pre-eminent American writers of the nineteenth century.

Louis Menand (born 1952) is a Pulitzer Prize-winning American literary critic and professor of English at Harvard University.

Ezra Pound (1885–1972) was an American expatriate poet and critic. As well known for his editing as for his poetry, he discovered and published major American poets, and founded the Imagist school of poetry, which stressed concreteness of visual description and played a defining role in literary modernism.

I. A. Richards (1893–1979) was a British poet and scholar. Richards is best known for helping to found the New Criticism movement through his teaching and pedagogical work at the University of Cambridge and Harvard University.

Christopher Ricks (born 1933) is a British literary critic and scholar, with a particular interest in poetry.

Josiah Royce (1855–1916) was an American philosopher who taught at Harvard University for many years. In his early career, he was a leading proponent of absolute idealism, the view that all aspects of reality are unified in a single all-encompassing consciousness (such as a higher power); he later revised his view and argued for "absolute pragmatism," the view that reality is a universe of signs interpreted by a community of minds.

Bertrand Russell (1872–1970) was a British philosopher best known for his work on mathematical logic and analytic philosophy. Russell is generally recognized as one of the founders of modern analytic philosophy.

William Shakespeare (1564–1616) was an English playwright and poet. His best-known works include *Romeo and Juliet, A Midsummer Night's Dream* and *Hamlet* among many other plays, as well as his sonnets. He worked as an actor and a writer in London during the rule of Elizabeth I, but his reputation far exceeds those of his contemporaries, and his influence on literature in English extends to the present day.

Rupert Shortt is a London-based writer and editor. He is Religion Editor at the *Times Literary Supplement,* and author of five books, including *Rowan's Rule: The Biography of the Archbishop* and *Benedict XVI: Commander of the Faith.*

Gertrude Stein (1874–1946) was an American poet, playwright, and novelist. She became an integral member of the circle of Anglo-American writers living and working in Paris during the first decades of the twentieth century, including F. Scott Fitzgerald and Ernest Hemingway. She is best known for her poetic experimentation with the linear and narrative conventions of nineteenth-century poetry.

Rowan Williams (born 1950) was Archbishop of Canterbury (the supreme head of the Church of England) from 2002 to 2012. He is also a noted theologian and literary scholar and is currently Master of Magdalene College, Cambridge.

William Carlos Williams (1883–1963) was an American poet known for experimental, vivid, often domestic poetry and for his conventional employment as a doctor.

Leonard Woolf (1880–1969) was a writer, publisher, and critic belonging to the Bloomsbury Group. He discovered and promoted many of London's leading writers in his role as co-publisher—with his wife, the novelist Virginia Woolf—at the Hogarth Press.

Virginia Woolf (1882–1941) was an English novelist, publisher, and critic, whose experimentation with the form of the novel had a major impact on the modernist movement in literature. Woolf is generally regarded as the most significant member of the Bloomsbury Group and is best known for her novels *Mrs. Dalloway* (1925) and *To the Lighthouse* (1927).

William Wordsworth (1770–1850) was one of the major poets of the Romantic movement in literature. With Samuel Taylor Coleridge, he helped to launch and define the Romantic movement in English poetry. Wordsworth is best known for *Lyrical Ballads* (1798, with Coleridge) and his long poem *The Prelude*.

WORKS CITED

WORKS CITED

Altieri, Charles. "Eliot's impact on twentieth-century Anglo-American poetry." In *The Cambridge Companion to T. S. Eliot*, edited by A. David Moody, 189–209. Cambridge: Cambridge University Press, 1994.

"Theorizing emotions in Eliot's poetry and poetics." In *Gender, Desire and Sexuality in T. S. Eliot*, edited by Cassandra Laity and Nancy K. Gish, 150–174. Cambridge: Cambridge University Press, 2004.

Atkins, G. Douglas. *Eliot and the Essay: From* The Sacred Wood *to* Four Quartets. Waco: Baylor University Press, 2010.

Brooker, Jewel Spears. *T. S. Eliot: The Contemporary Reviews*. American Critical Archives Series. Cambridge: Cambridge University Press, 2004.

Domestico, Anthony. "The Sacred Wood." In *The Modernism Lab at Yale University*, edited by Pericles Lewis, 2010. Accessed August 29, 2014. http://modernism.research.yale.edu/wiki/index.php/The_Sacred_Wood.

Eliot, Thomas Stearns. *The Sacred Wood: Essays on Poetry and Criticism.* 2nd edition. London: Faber & Faber, 1997.

For Lancelot Andrewes: Essays on Style and Order. London: Faber & Faber, 1970.

Knowledge and Experience in the Philosophy of F. H. Bradley. London: Faber & Faber, 1964.

To Criticize the Critic and Other Writings. Edited by Valerie Eliot. New York: Farrar, Straus, and Giroux, 1965.

The Letters of T. S. Eliot, Vols. 1–4, edited by Valerie Eliot, Hugh Haughton, and John Haffenden. London: Faber & Faber, 2011–2013.

Harding, Jason. *The Criterion: Cultural Politics and Periodical Networks in Inter-War Britain*. Oxford: Oxford University Press, 2002.

Huisman, David. "Title and Subject in *The Sacred Wood.*" *Essays in Criticism XXXIX* [3] (1989): 217–233.

Julius, Anthony. *T. S. Eliot, anti-Semitism, and literary form*. London: Thames & Hudson, 2003.

Kirk, Russell. *Eliot and His Age: T. S. Eliot's Moral Imagination in the Twentieth Century*. Wilmington: Intercollegiate Studies Institute, 2008.

Lewis, Pericles. *The Cambridge Introduction to Modernism*. Cambridge: Cambridge University Press, 2007.

Menand, Louis. *Discovering Modernism: T. S. Eliot and His Context.* 2nd edition. New York: Oxford University Press, 2007.

Rabaté, Jean-Michel. "Tradition and T. S. Eliot." In *The Cambridge Companion to T. S. Eliot*, edited by A. David Moody, 210–222. Cambridge: Cambridge University Press, 1994.

Ricks, Christopher. *T. S. Eliot and Prejudice.* Berkeley: University of California Press, 1988.

Scott, Peter Dale. "The social critic and his discontents." In *The Cambridge Companion to T. S. Eliot,* edited by A. David Moody, 60–76. Cambridge: Cambridge University Press, 1994.

Shortt, Rupert. *Rowan's Rule: The Biography of the Archbishop of Canterbury.* Grand Rapids: Eerdmanns Publishing, 2009.

Shusterman, Richard. "Eliot as philosopher." In *The Cambridge Companion to T. S. Eliot*, edited by A. David Moody, 31–47. Cambridge: Cambridge University Press, 1994.

Sigg, Eric. "Eliot as a product of America." In *The Cambridge Companion to T. S. Eliot*, edited by A. David Moody, 14–30. Cambridge: Cambridge University Press, 1994.

Surette, Leon. *Dreams of a Totalitarian Utopia: Literary Modernism and Politics.* Toronto: McGill-Queen's University Press, 2011.

Williams, Rowan. *Dostoevsky: Language, Faith, and Fiction.* Waco: Baylor University Press, 2008.

THE MACAT LIBRARY
BY DISCIPLINE

AFRICANA STUDIES

Chinua Achebe's *An Image of Africa: Racism in Conrad's Heart of Darkness*
W. E. B. Du Bois's *The Souls of Black Folk*
Zora Neale Huston's *Characteristics of Negro Expression*
Martin Luther King Jr's *Why We Can't Wait*
Toni Morrison's *Playing in the Dark: Whiteness in the American Literary Imagination*

ANTHROPOLOGY

Arjun Appadurai's *Modernity at Large: Cultural Dimensions of Globalisation*
Philippe Ariès's *Centuries of Childhood*
Franz Boas's *Race, Language and Culture*
Kim Chan & Renée Mauborgne's *Blue Ocean Strategy*
Jared Diamond's *Guns, Germs & Steel: the Fate of Human Societies*
Jared Diamond's *Collapse: How Societies Choose to Fail or Survive*
E. E. Evans-Pritchard's *Witchcraft, Oracles and Magic Among the Azande*
James Ferguson's *The Anti-Politics Machine*
Clifford Geertz's *The Interpretation of Cultures*
David Graeber's *Debt: the First 5000 Years*
Karen Ho's *Liquidated: An Ethnography of Wall Street*
Geert Hofstede's *Culture's Consequences: Comparing Values, Behaviors, Institutes and Organizations across Nations*
Claude Lévi-Strauss's *Structural Anthropology*
Jay Macleod's *Ain't No Makin' It: Aspirations and Attainment in a Low-Income Neighborhood*
Saba Mahmood's *The Politics of Piety: The Islamic Revival and the Feminist Subject*
Marcel Mauss's *The Gift*

BUSINESS

Jean Lave & Etienne Wenger's *Situated Learning*
Theodore Levitt's *Marketing Myopia*
Burton G. Malkiel's *A Random Walk Down Wall Street*
Douglas McGregor's *The Human Side of Enterprise*
Michael Porter's *Competitive Strategy: Creating and Sustaining Superior Performance*
John Kotter's *Leading Change*
C. K. Prahalad & Gary Hamel's *The Core Competence of the Corporation*

CRIMINOLOGY

Michelle Alexander's *The New Jim Crow: Mass Incarceration in the Age of Colorblindness*
Michael R. Gottfredson & Travis Hirschi's *A General Theory of Crime*
Richard Herrnstein & Charles A. Murray's *The Bell Curve: Intelligence and Class Structure in American Life*
Elizabeth Loftus's *Eyewitness Testimony*
Jay Macleod's *Ain't No Makin' It: Aspirations and Attainment in a Low-Income Neighborhood*
Philip Zimbardo's *The Lucifer Effect*

ECONOMICS

Janet Abu-Lughod's *Before European Hegemony*
Ha-Joon Chang's *Kicking Away the Ladder*
David Brion Davis's *The Problem of Slavery in the Age of Revolution*
Milton Friedman's *The Role of Monetary Policy*
Milton Friedman's *Capitalism and Freedom*
David Graeber's *Debt: the First 5000 Years*
Friedrich Hayek's *The Road to Serfdom*
Karen Ho's *Liquidated: An Ethnography of Wall Street*

John Maynard Keynes's *The General Theory of Employment, Interest and Money*
Charles P. Kindleberger's *Manias, Panics and Crashes*
Robert Lucas's *Why Doesn't Capital Flow from Rich to Poor Countries?*
Burton G. Malkiel's *A Random Walk Down Wall Street*
Thomas Robert Malthus's *An Essay on the Principle of Population*
Karl Marx's *Capital*
Thomas Piketty's *Capital in the Twenty-First Century*
Amartya Sen's *Development as Freedom*
Adam Smith's *The Wealth of Nations*
Nassim Nicholas Taleb's *The Black Swan: The Impact of the Highly Improbable*
Amos Tversky's & Daniel Kahneman's *Judgment under Uncertainty: Heuristics and Biases*
Mahbub Ul Haq's *Reflections on Human Development*
Max Weber's *The Protestant Ethic and the Spirit of Capitalism*

FEMINISM AND GENDER STUDIES

Judith Butler's *Gender Trouble*
Simone De Beauvoir's *The Second Sex*
Michel Foucault's *History of Sexuality*
Betty Friedan's *The Feminine Mystique*
Saba Mahmood's *The Politics of Piety: The Islamic Revival and the Feminist Subject*
Joan Wallach Scott's *Gender and the Politics of History*
Mary Wollstonecraft's *A Vindication of the Rights of Woman*
Virginia Woolf's *A Room of One's Own*

GEOGRAPHY

The Brundtland Report's *Our Common Future*
Rachel Carson's *Silent Spring*
Charles Darwin's *On the Origin of Species*
James Ferguson's *The Anti-Politics Machine*
Jane Jacobs's *The Death and Life of Great American Cities*
James Lovelock's *Gaia: A New Look at Life on Earth*
Amartya Sen's *Development as Freedom*
Mathis Wackernagel & William Rees's *Our Ecological Footprint*

HISTORY

Janet Abu-Lughod's *Before European Hegemony*
Benedict Anderson's *Imagined Communities*
Bernard Bailyn's *The Ideological Origins of the American Revolution*
Hanna Batatu's *The Old Social Classes And The Revolutionary Movements Of Iraq*
Christopher Browning's *Ordinary Men: Reserve Police Batallion 101 and the Final Solution in Poland*
Edmund Burke's *Reflections on the Revolution in France*
William Cronon's *Nature's Metropolis: Chicago And The Great West*
Alfred W. Crosby's *The Columbian Exchange*
Hamid Dabashi's *Iran: A People Interrupted*
David Brion Davis's *The Problem of Slavery in the Age of Revolution*
Nathalie Zemon Davis's *The Return of Martin Guerre*
Jared Diamond's *Guns, Germs & Steel: the Fate of Human Societies*
Frank Dikotter's *Mao's Great Famine*
John W Dower's *War Without Mercy: Race And Power In The Pacific War*
W. E. B. Du Bois's *The Souls of Black Folk*
Richard J. Evans's *In Defence of History*
Lucien Febvre's *The Problem of Unbelief in the 16th Century*
Sheila Fitzpatrick's *Everyday Stalinism*

Eric Foner's *Reconstruction: America's Unfinished Revolution, 1863-1877*
Michel Foucault's *Discipline and Punish*
Michel Foucault's *History of Sexuality*
Francis Fukuyama's *The End of History and the Last Man*
John Lewis Gaddis's *We Now Know: Rethinking Cold War History*
Ernest Gellner's *Nations and Nationalism*
Eugene Genovese's *Roll, Jordan, Roll: The World the Slaves Made*
Carlo Ginzburg's *The Night Battles*
Daniel Goldhagen's *Hitler's Willing Executioners*
Jack Goldstone's *Revolution and Rebellion in the Early Modern World*
Antonio Gramsci's *The Prison Notebooks*
Alexander Hamilton, John Jay & James Madison's *The Federalist Papers*
Christopher Hill's *The World Turned Upside Down*
Carole Hillenbrand's *The Crusades: Islamic Perspectives*
Thomas Hobbes's *Leviathan*
Eric Hobsbawm's *The Age Of Revolution*
John A. Hobson's *Imperialism: A Study*
Albert Hourani's *History of the Arab Peoples*
Samuel P. Huntington's *The Clash of Civilizations and the Remaking of World Order*
C. L. R. James's *The Black Jacobins*
Tony Judt's *Postwar: A History of Europe Since 1945*
Ernst Kantorowicz's *The King's Two Bodies: A Study in Medieval Political Theology*
Paul Kennedy's *The Rise and Fall of the Great Powers*
Ian Kershaw's *The "Hitler Myth": Image and Reality in the Third Reich*
John Maynard Keynes's *The General Theory of Employment, Interest and Money*
Charles P. Kindleberger's *Manias, Panics and Crashes*
Martin Luther King Jr's *Why We Can't Wait*
Henry Kissinger's *World Order: Reflections on the Character of Nations and the Course of History*
Thomas Kuhn's *The Structure of Scientific Revolutions*
Georges Lefebvre's *The Coming of the French Revolution*
John Locke's *Two Treatises of Government*
Niccolò Machiavelli's *The Prince*
Thomas Robert Malthus's *An Essay on the Principle of Population*
Mahmood Mamdani's *Citizen and Subject: Contemporary Africa And The Legacy Of Late Colonialism*
Karl Marx's *Capital*
Stanley Milgram's *Obedience to Authority*
John Stuart Mill's *On Liberty*
Thomas Paine's *Common Sense*
Thomas Paine's *Rights of Man*
Geoffrey Parker's *Global Crisis: War, Climate Change and Catastrophe in the Seventeenth Century*
Jonathan Riley-Smith's *The First Crusade and the Idea of Crusading*
Jean-Jacques Rousseau's *The Social Contract*
Joan Wallach Scott's *Gender and the Politics of History*
Theda Skocpol's *States and Social Revolutions*
Adam Smith's *The Wealth of Nations*
Timothy Snyder's *Bloodlands: Europe Between Hitler and Stalin*
Sun Tzu's *The Art of War*
Keith Thomas's *Religion and the Decline of Magic*
Thucydides's *The History of the Peloponnesian War*
Frederick Jackson Turner's *The Significance of the Frontier in American History*
Odd Arne Westad's *The Global Cold War: Third World Interventions And The Making Of Our Times*

LITERATURE

Chinua Achebe's *An Image of Africa: Racism in Conrad's Heart of Darkness*
Roland Barthes's *Mythologies*
Homi K. Bhabha's *The Location of Culture*
Judith Butler's *Gender Trouble*
Simone De Beauvoir's *The Second Sex*
Ferdinand De Saussure's *Course in General Linguistics*
T. S. Eliot's *The Sacred Wood: Essays on Poetry and Criticism*
Zora Neale Huston's *Characteristics of Negro Expression*
Toni Morrison's *Playing in the Dark: Whiteness in the American Literary Imagination*
Edward Said's *Orientalism*
Gayatri Chakravorty Spivak's *Can the Subaltern Speak?*
Mary Wollstonecraft's *A Vindication of the Rights of Women*
Virginia Woolf's *A Room of One's Own*

PHILOSOPHY

Elizabeth Anscombe's *Modern Moral Philosophy*
Hannah Arendt's *The Human Condition*
Aristotle's *Metaphysics*
Aristotle's *Nicomachean Ethics*
Edmund Gettier's *Is Justified True Belief Knowledge?*
Georg Wilhelm Friedrich Hegel's *Phenomenology of Spirit*
David Hume's *Dialogues Concerning Natural Religion*
David Hume's *The Enquiry for Human Understanding*
Immanuel Kant's *Religion within the Boundaries of Mere Reason*
Immanuel Kant's *Critique of Pure Reason*
Søren Kierkegaard's *The Sickness Unto Death*
Søren Kierkegaard's *Fear and Trembling*
C. S. Lewis's *The Abolition of Man*
Alasdair MacIntyre's *After Virtue*
Marcus Aurelius's *Meditations*
Friedrich Nietzsche's *On the Genealogy of Morality*
Friedrich Nietzsche's *Beyond Good and Evil*
Plato's *Republic*
Plato's *Symposium*
Jean-Jacques Rousseau's *The Social Contract*
Gilbert Ryle's *The Concept of Mind*
Baruch Spinoza's *Ethics*
Sun Tzu's *The Art of War*
Ludwig Wittgenstein's *Philosophical Investigations*

POLITICS

Benedict Anderson's *Imagined Communities*
Aristotle's *Politics*
Bernard Bailyn's *The Ideological Origins of the American Revolution*
Edmund Burke's *Reflections on the Revolution in France*
John C. Calhoun's *A Disquisition on Government*
Ha-Joon Chang's *Kicking Away the Ladder*
Hamid Dabashi's *Iran: A People Interrupted*
Hamid Dabashi's *Theology of Discontent: The Ideological Foundation of the Islamic Revolution in Iran*
Robert Dahl's *Democracy and its Critics*
Robert Dahl's *Who Governs?*
David Brion Davis's *The Problem of Slavery in the Age of Revolution*

The Macat Library By Discipline

Alexis De Tocqueville's *Democracy in America*
James Ferguson's *The Anti-Politics Machine*
Frank Dikotter's *Mao's Great Famine*
Sheila Fitzpatrick's *Everyday Stalinism*
Eric Foner's *Reconstruction: America's Unfinished Revolution, 1863-1877*
Milton Friedman's *Capitalism and Freedom*
Francis Fukuyama's *The End of History and the Last Man*
John Lewis Gaddis's *We Now Know: Rethinking Cold War History*
Ernest Gellner's *Nations and Nationalism*
David Graeber's *Debt: the First 5000 Years*
Antonio Gramsci's *The Prison Notebooks*
Alexander Hamilton, John Jay & James Madison's *The Federalist Papers*
Friedrich Hayek's *The Road to Serfdom*
Christopher Hill's *The World Turned Upside Down*
Thomas Hobbes's *Leviathan*
John A. Hobson's *Imperialism: A Study*
Samuel P. Huntington's *The Clash of Civilizations and the Remaking of World Order*
Tony Judt's *Postwar: A History of Europe Since 1945*
David C. Kang's *China Rising: Peace, Power and Order in East Asia*
Paul Kennedy's *The Rise and Fall of Great Powers*
Robert Keohane's *After Hegemony*
Martin Luther King Jr.'s *Why We Can't Wait*
Henry Kissinger's *World Order: Reflections on the Character of Nations and the Course of History*
John Locke's *Two Treatises of Government*
Niccolò Machiavelli's *The Prince*
Thomas Robert Malthus's *An Essay on the Principle of Population*
Mahmood Mamdani's *Citizen and Subject: Contemporary Africa And The Legacy Of Late Colonialism*
Karl Marx's *Capital*
John Stuart Mill's *On Liberty*
John Stuart Mill's *Utilitarianism*
Hans Morgenthau's *Politics Among Nations*
Thomas Paine's *Common Sense*
Thomas Paine's *Rights of Man*
Thomas Piketty's *Capital in the Twenty-First Century*
Robert D. Putman's *Bowling Alone*
John Rawls's *Theory of Justice*
Jean-Jacques Rousseau's *The Social Contract*
Theda Skocpol's *States and Social Revolutions*
Adam Smith's *The Wealth of Nations*
Sun Tzu's *The Art of War*
Henry David Thoreau's *Civil Disobedience*
Thucydides's *The History of the Peloponnesian War*
Kenneth Waltz's *Theory of International Politics*
Max Weber's *Politics as a Vocation*
Odd Arne Westad's *The Global Cold War: Third World Interventions And The Making Of Our Times*

POSTCOLONIAL STUDIES

Roland Barthes's *Mythologies*
Frantz Fanon's *Black Skin, White Masks*
Homi K. Bhabha's *The Location of Culture*
Gustavo Gutiérrez's *A Theology of Liberation*
Edward Said's *Orientalism*
Gayatri Chakravorty Spivak's *Can the Subaltern Speak?*

PSYCHOLOGY

Gordon Allport's *The Nature of Prejudice*
Alan Baddeley & Graham Hitch's *Aggression: A Social Learning Analysis*
Albert Bandura's *Aggression: A Social Learning Analysis*
Leon Festinger's *A Theory of Cognitive Dissonance*
Sigmund Freud's *The Interpretation of Dreams*
Betty Friedan's *The Feminine Mystique*
Michael R. Gottfredson & Travis Hirschi's *A General Theory of Crime*
Eric Hoffer's *The True Believer: Thoughts on the Nature of Mass Movements*
William James's *Principles of Psychology*
Elizabeth Loftus's *Eyewitness Testimony*
A. H. Maslow's *A Theory of Human Motivation*
Stanley Milgram's *Obedience to Authority*
Steven Pinker's *The Better Angels of Our Nature*
Oliver Sacks's *The Man Who Mistook His Wife For a Hat*
Richard Thaler & Cass Sunstein's *Nudge: Improving Decisions About Health, Wealth and Happiness*
Amos Tversky's *Judgment under Uncertainty: Heuristics and Biases*
Philip Zimbardo's *The Lucifer Effect*

SCIENCE

Rachel Carson's *Silent Spring*
William Cronon's *Nature's Metropolis: Chicago And The Great West*
Alfred W. Crosby's *The Columbian Exchange*
Charles Darwin's *On the Origin of Species*
Richard Dawkin's *The Selfish Gene*
Thomas Kuhn's *The Structure of Scientific Revolutions*
Geoffrey Parker's *Global Crisis: War, Climate Change and Catastrophe in the Seventeenth Century*
Mathis Wackernagel & William Rees's *Our Ecological Footprint*

SOCIOLOGY

Michelle Alexander's *The New Jim Crow: Mass Incarceration in the Age of Colorblindness*
Gordon Allport's *The Nature of Prejudice*
Albert Bandura's *Aggression: A Social Learning Analysis*
Hanna Batatu's *The Old Social Classes And The Revolutionary Movements Of Iraq*
Ha-Joon Chang's *Kicking Away the Ladder*
W. E. B. Du Bois's *The Souls of Black Folk*
Émile Durkheim's *On Suicide*
Frantz Fanon's *Black Skin, White Masks*
Frantz Fanon's *The Wretched of the Earth*
Eric Foner's *Reconstruction: America's Unfinished Revolution, 1863-1877*
Eugene Genovese's *Roll, Jordan, Roll: The World the Slaves Made*
Jack Goldstone's *Revolution and Rebellion in the Early Modern World*
Antonio Gramsci's *The Prison Notebooks*
Richard Herrnstein & Charles A Murray's *The Bell Curve: Intelligence and Class Structure in American Life*
Eric Hoffer's *The True Believer: Thoughts on the Nature of Mass Movements*
Jane Jacobs's *The Death and Life of Great American Cities*
Robert Lucas's *Why Doesn't Capital Flow from Rich to Poor Countries?*
Jay Macleod's *Ain't No Makin' It: Aspirations and Attainment in a Low Income Neighborhood*
Elaine May's *Homeward Bound: American Families in the Cold War Era*
Douglas McGregor's *The Human Side of Enterprise*
C. Wright Mills's *The Sociological Imagination*

Thomas Piketty's *Capital in the Twenty-First Century*
Robert D. Putman's *Bowling Alone*
David Riesman's *The Lonely Crowd: A Study of the Changing American Character*
Edward Said's *Orientalism*
Joan Wallach Scott's *Gender and the Politics of History*
Theda Skocpol's *States and Social Revolutions*
Max Weber's *The Protestant Ethic and the Spirit of Capitalism*

THEOLOGY

Augustine's *Confessions*
Benedict's *Rule of St Benedict*
Gustavo Gutiérrez's *A Theology of Liberation*
Carole Hillenbrand's *The Crusades: Islamic Perspectives*
David Hume's *Dialogues Concerning Natural Religion*
Immanuel Kant's *Religion within the Boundaries of Mere Reason*
Ernst Kantorowicz's *The King's Two Bodies: A Study in Medieval Political Theology*
Søren Kierkegaard's *The Sickness Unto Death*
C. S. Lewis's *The Abolition of Man*
Saba Mahmood's *The Politics of Piety: The Islamic Revival and the Feminist Subject*
Baruch Spinoza's *Ethics*
Keith Thomas's *Religion and the Decline of Magic*

COMING SOON

Chris Argyris's *The Individual and the Organisation*
Seyla Benhabib's *The Rights of Others*
Walter Benjamin's *The Work Of Art in the Age of Mechanical Reproduction*
John Berger's *Ways of Seeing*
Pierre Bourdieu's *Outline of a Theory of Practice*
Mary Douglas's *Purity and Danger*
Roland Dworkin's *Taking Rights Seriously*
James G. March's *Exploration and Exploitation in Organisational Learning*
Ikujiro Nonaka's *A Dynamic Theory of Organizational Knowledge Creation*
Griselda Pollock's *Vision and Difference*
Amartya Sen's *Inequality Re-Examined*
Susan Sontag's *On Photography*
Yasser Tabbaa's *The Transformation of Islamic Art*
Ludwig von Mises's *Theory of Money and Credit*

Macat Disciplines

Access the greatest ideas and thinkers across entire disciplines, including

TOTALITARIANISM

Sheila Fitzpatrick's, *Everyday Stalinism*
Ian Kershaw's, *The "Hitler Myth"*
Timothy Snyder's, *Bloodlands*

Macat analyses are available from all good bookshops and libraries.

Access hundreds of analyses through one, multimedia tool.
Join free for one month **library.macat.com**

Printed in the United States
by Baker & Taylor Publisher Services